"Reading *A Gentle Return*, I felt seen, heard, and celebrated as I navigate womanhood. While I am not a mother, I am a daughter, sister and friend. Within the intimate essays shared, I found myself relating to the author's experience in ways that I had not yet been able to communicate with others because I had not yet found the language to describe certain facets of my pain, discernment and joy. These essays helped me discover the words I needed to begin my reflection and, eventually, my gentle return to my true, authentic self. This book serves as a helpful guide that reminds us that there is actual power in a shared experience, should we have the courage to invite others into the privacy of our hearts and thoughts.

While I laughed and smiled through some essays, what surprised me the most was the new perspective I now find myself considering in my relationship with my mother. She is a woman, too. She is a daughter, too. My mother has her own set of hopes and heartaches that have slowly shaped her into the woman she is today. I find myself, more than ever before, considering how her choices, challenges and crises have charted a course for the life she leads and how she, too, may need grace, encouragement and sisterhood to make her own gentle return. As this book reminds us, mothers deserve to be endeared in their quest for empathy, exhilaration and enlightenment. This new perspective—to truly view my mother as her own woman with her own desires and thoughts—is a gift from the author for which I am most grateful."

—**Melissa Correa**, *experience enthusiast, dream manifester, cheerleader to my friends and family, hopeful romantic*

"Catia dives head-first into the complexities of being a woman. At times, *A Gentle Return* spoke straight to my soul—a gasp here and there with me thinking, 'Wow, how could she have had the same thought as me?' And other times left me feeling more empathy for situations that haven't happened to me directly but I know have happened to women I love. *A Gentle Return* gives me the confidence to know that we are all a combination of shiny and tarnished, and the blessing is owning it and sharing our stories. I appreciate how honest and brave this collection is. It was a gentle hug full of self-help, self-reflection, and ultimately self-love. This book could only be written by someone self-assured and coming from a place wanting to help others. Someone with the confidence to say, 'Here, I'll go first and tell you all about it.'"

—**Tracy Bullion**, *devoted wife, grateful mother, friend, creative*

"*A Gentle Return* is a beautifully written book about life's challenges. From the moment I started reading, I was captivated by Catia's strength to share her experiences that, as a woman, you are taught not to speak about. Catia's bravery has created a new sense of bravery in me. Catia has taught me that I can be a great mother and daughter but also carry trauma that takes time to heal. Catia has also taught me that I am a great mother who doesn't need to do it all. Showing up for myself and my family doesn't need to follow the rules society has established for me; sometimes, it's just a matter of being present. Each story left me with a sense of empowerment and encouraged me to reflect on my journey from childhood to adulthood to motherhood. This book had me crying tears of happiness and sadness. It left me yearning for a hug from my mom, making me realize that I will always need my mother no matter where I am or what I'm doing. It left me with feelings of hope in mending torn relationships while letting me know it's okay to take time to heal myself. *A Gentle Return* is a thought-provoking and heartfelt reminder of what it truly means to be powerful and to love yourself."

—**Ashley Hernandez,** *adoring mother, good listener, lifelong learner, birth trauma survivor*

"If the phrase 'I see you' was a book, this is it. Tears streamed down my cheeks and blurred my eyes as it became evident that the tensions, tangles, twists, turns, and triumphs I've experienced in my own life and within my own heart are, in fact, shared amongst all women. The details of our stories may vary, but the themes connect us all. Reading this felt like a gentle hug that made me feel a lot less alone. Catia's voice is like a balm for all the old wounds of all my younger selves. Perhaps the biggest gift in reading this is the assurance that every version of me that ever ran away from authenticity is still worthy, welcome, and invited back home."

—**Janelle Velo**, *nature lover, biological mother, foster mother, Conscious Parenting Coach*

"*A Gentle Return* is a beautiful reminder of the powerful interconnectedness that women share. This book masterfully illustrates the common threads that weave through our stories. A heartwarming read that left me feeling inspired and uplifted.

I can't tell you how wonderful this book is. Thank you for writing it and being so open and vulnerable in sharing your experiences. Many emotions were brought to the surface as I personally related to so much of what I was reading. I'm getting a copy for every woman in my family!"

—**Leigh Gomez**, *mom, dancer, hypnotherapist, and Conscious Parenting Coach*

"I couldn't put it down; Catia's stories felt like my stories, too. *A Gentle Return* is real, raw, and vulnerable. Growing up in our Hispanic culture, we are taught not to share, not to show emotions, and not to talk about our feelings. But we do have these experiences, and it's important that we share them with each other. This book encouraged me to look at my relationship with my mother, in contrast to my relationship with my daughter, and how now, as a mother of a daughter, I see things and understand my own mother more. I felt like I was having a conversation with Catia. I loved it."

—**Gloria Rodriguez**, *fitness enthusiast, licensed radiology technician, student in the social work program, mother*

"*A Gentle Return* came at an ideal time in my life. What resonated with me the most was how we, as women, are so attuned to what is needed and expected of us and how we adhere to those needs and expectations. But I have learned to put myself first, which *A Gentle Return* encouraged me to do. Catia is an excellent storyteller; her stories shed light on experiences I knew had impacted me but could not put my finger on."

—**Lisa Garcia**, *friend, woman, trauma survivor, hopeful human*

"*A Gentle Return* is about taking a step back in life to reflect on it and let yourself be moved. While reading, I wondered how truly in touch with myself I have been throughout my life, if at all. I'm not perfect; I definitely don't fit society's standards, and I fall short even of my expectations. Catia's words encouraged me to see and nurture the parts of me that feel inadequate, to cultivate a sense of agency, and to love myself well."

—**Maria Mohamed,** *learner, daughter, joy seeker, future therapist*

"From the very first page, I felt a strong connection to Catia and her stories. It took me to a place of reflection and contemplation in my own life. It encouraged me to view my life through a different and deeper lens. This collection of stories helped me lean toward gratitude and compassion for what I have experienced and has moved me toward healing. *A Gentle Return* ignited a sense of courage and confidence to live into my passion and abundance. I have regained my trust in God. Thank you, Catia. Thank you for showing up."

—**Priyanka Priya,** *mother, daughter, Conscious Parenting Coach, seeker*

a
gentle
return

a gentle return

A Mother's Meditations on Embodying Fulfillment, Pleasure, and Worth

Catia Hernández Holm

Grace Strategies, LLC
Austin, Texas

First edition 2023

Cover and book design by Sheila Parr

Cover images © Shutterstock: Michael M.H. Ng,
agsandrew, and Twins Design Studio
Interior art © iStockphoto: Yuliya Mikhaylovskay
and Daria Grushina

Hardcover: 978-0-9983782-1-3

Paperback: 978-0-9983782-5-1

Ebook: 978-0-9983782-3-7

Published by Grace Strategies, LLC

www.catiaholm.com

Behind every strong woman
is her sacred feminine bloodline.
—Indigenous Proverb

For Alexandra and Luciana
You are my dream come true.
Your hearts and spirits inspire me.
I am so proud of you, and I delight
in you every single day.

For Mom
I am because you are.
—African Proverb

You taught me how to be strong, love well, and
create a house that feels like a home.
I love you.

a gentle return

A Mother's Meditations on Embodying Fulfillment, Pleasure, and Worth

Catia Hernández Holm

CONTENTS

A NOTE FROM THE AUTHOR xix

INTRODUCTION: ACCEPTING THE INVITATION . . . 1

ESSAYS:

Welita 9

The Trauma of Childbirth 17

Mom 31

Aggrieved 43

Misty 55

Las Mujeres Increibles 63

Desperti 75

Choosing Slow 83

Mama, what is beauty? 93

My Hair, My Body 99

You Are My Bucket List 105

Hands On Cheeks 117

Cold Plunge 127

The Protocol 135

Guapo Leaving Town 143

Sensuality 151

The Unfolding 163

Karaoke 175

CONCLUSION: TIME TO RETURN 183

ACKNOWLEDGMENTS 191

BIBLIOGRAPHY 195

ABOUT THE AUTHOR 196

A NOTE FROM THE AUTHOR

This book is about embracing and valuing our gifts, mysteries, and wholeness as women.

The stories I share in this book reflect my viewpoint to the best of my memory's capacity.

While some people in this book are referred to by name,

Anthony, my husband
Alexandra, our oldest daughter
Luciana, our youngest daughter

the names of others and some details have been changed to preserve their privacy.

It is not my intention to speak for all women but to offer the intimate perspective of one woman, this woman, in hopes that other women feel seen, validated, and encouraged.

Introduction

ACCEPTING *the* INVITATION

Mothers teach their daughters how to brush their teeth and make turkey sandwiches, and mothers also teach their daughters how to love, grow, and survive. The relationship is infinitely sacred, complex, and intertwined. As women, we teach each other how to define success and handle power, relationships, money, stress, romance, body image, and careers. As daughters, we look to our mothers for guidance on how to behave, think, and become. We absorb the qualities and energies our mothers exude—for better or worse. In many ways, we shape each other.

If you're reading this book, you've likely arrived at this precious middle season of life: You are a mother to young children, yet you are also a daughter.

You are the living bridge.

I, too, am a mother and a daughter. And from time to time, I see and feel that so many of us have tenuous relationships with the women in our lives. So many of us experience the world through a fractured lens, never really appreciating the beauty of who we are or those around us, maybe because our hearts were wounded and never healed. So many of us feel unseen, unsupported, and unloved—sometimes, we are unsure why.

Our stories and our reasons vary, but we all walk with hurt.

Throughout our lives, we endure emotional, psychological, and physical traumas. We lead busy lives, give birth to babies, reach for validation, run other people's races, and serve until we are empty. Over time, we become disconnected from our bodies, internal experience, and knowing. In the everyday hustle, we forget just how valuable our internal experience is. What would it look like to feel whole? What would it feel like to reclaim our stories and reconnect to our inner knowing?

Most of us are taught that success lives outside of us. It's no wonder many of us feel like we're doing it wrong. No wonder we have mean train conductors in our minds, yelling at us to keep going, go faster, and move! We are taught to view success through the lens of heroes, through the lens of men. We learned that success looks like a well-paying job, a fancy house, vacations, a happy marriage, and children—all getting 10% bigger and better by the year. We are taught that there is a baseline, and then there is the skyline. Reaching the skyline is the pinnacle; you can only get there if you work hard enough. But what about the heroine's journey?

Our hearts feel good with slobbery baby kisses and having bottomless pots of coffee with girlfriends until we run out of things to talk about—but since those things aren't award-worthy markers of external success, we prioritize them less. We value them less.

As women, there is something so primal and present in us that we can look inward instead of outward to find meaning. And, every day, we can make decisions that get us closer to that feeling of fulfillment, of peace. We can drop into the center of our lives instead of floating above them and wishing them into another season.

We can move beyond the hollowness of perpetual striving and instead toward alignment with our true purpose. We can redefine and reimagine what it means to create a meaningful life by exploring our deepest depths, giving ourselves permission to ask hard questions, and melting into the new truths we find in the answers.

The moment I realized I had been striving for someone else's definition of success—leaving my spirit arid and wrung out—I realized I needed deep nourishment. There had been a part of me that I had been neglecting, and I instinctively knew the salve would be turning toward it and, maybe one day, embracing it. I realized I wanted to look backward and find my mother, look forward and hold on to my children, and look inward to re-align myself with my heart. I can still feel the power of this sudden and strong call back to myself and how it changed everything inside me.

As women, we are dynamic; we are living bridges, bridging the gap between generations, between characteristics, and between the physical and spiritual realms. Early on, we absorb a limited definition of who and what we should be and then work diligently to uphold that standard. However, it never feels quite right because it's stagnant; it doesn't give us enough space to grow, experience, and thrive. I have begun to explore and define a *gentle return* to myself and my essence and what a gentle return means as a driving force in my life.

I had to reflect on where I came from to gently return to myself, surrender to the past, and embrace my wholeness. I had to get curious about who my mom was, how she was raised, and who her mother was. Instead of following the outside call of hustle and achievement, I answered the call of myself as the bridge. I began a *gentle return* to my true power, which meant a better understanding of my mother and two daughters and my role as the connective tissue between them. Who am I when I return to my true self and embody it?

I keep shedding layers, ideas, and beliefs as I keep learning, unfolding, and expanding. As I learn, I acquire a new belief and shed the old one until I learn more, and the shedding begins all over again. It's perpetual change. At times, the change is exhausting but always illuminating and rewarding. I write all that to share that this is a living book; these are living stories.

In these pages, you'll be able to see how the threads of our lives weave together and how they can be beautiful, but also how your thread—your experience—can be beautiful on its own, apart from the others.

We must explore and figure this out for ourselves. We must begin our own heroine's journey. We must play with it, fumble, and turn it on its head. We have to go far, run with it, and see how it stretches, pulls, frays, and maybe even breaks. And our discovery can't be forced, manipulated, or rushed—all in good time. Each story is a precise thread to do what you want to do with it.

This book explores the sacred relationships between the women who raised us, our mysterious selves, and the women we are raising. These essays are an intimate record of my reclaiming and gentle return to my wholeness and goodness. These essays are a series of offerings to invite you to embark on your gentle return.

I sincerely want to support you as you move toward embodying pleasure, fulfillment, worth, and satisfaction. I want you to experience your inner knowing and power and feel the full arc of your life as a woman.

These pages won't provide you with solutions or give you answers. Still, they will make another way available—the heroine's journey.

We must learn to use the gifts we are born with—to stretch wide and fly, sometimes to lay flat and offer ourselves as a bridge, and even sometimes to wrap like a warm cocoon around those we love. We must connect the inside with the outside and across the generations. We must breathe life into this precious middle season and experience its blessings.

May these pages support you in moving toward a life filled with pleasure, fulfillment, worth, and satisfaction. May these pages help you undertake a *gentle return* to your sense of goodness and wholeness.

I am with you.

Shall we?

Death has nothing to do with going away.
The sun sets. The moon sets. But they are not gone.
—Rumi

WELITA

It's 10:00 a.m. I'm standing in the kitchen, chopping overripe zucchini for dinner. After this morning's whirlwind, my feet are bare and uncomfortable from the leftover breadcrumbs. The girls are at school. Anthony, my husband, is working from home. The house is quiet enough for me to drink a hot coffee without reheating it.

My phone pings like it has a million times before, and I look down to scan the message. There it is. The news I have braced for so many times before has finally arrived. *She has died.* My Abuelita, my grandmother, has died. My first thought is my mom lost her mom. My second thought is I want to be there for my mom. When tragedy strikes, we want to be near, comforted, and together. Sometimes, we want, but don't know what.

We have people in our lives who are so constant that they become a beautiful thread weaving together our spirit, and when their bodies leave Earth, we are confronted with the knowledge that their loss will change us; we just don't know how.

Anthony walks in from the yard, having received the same text message, and, without saying a word, he sits in my blue velvet office chair, motioning for me. His lap and arms have held my sorrow so many times before. My chest is heaving—trying to process four decades of love. "She loved me so much," I bellow, "and I loved her so much."

Within 24 hours, I am in my childhood home with my mom. I'm middle-aged and comforted by being tethered to my mother. As I watch my mom walk across the living room, I feel a pit in my stomach, knowing my mom's tether is no longer.

Instead of leaning into grief, I leaned into planning. My Abuelita was my last living grandparent, so I was familiar with the rhythm of the rituals: A Catholic rosary, a funeral service, a burial, and all the hugs and tears in between. I decided to take charge of as much as possible to allow my family to grieve rather than plan, or maybe I wasn't ready to grieve. Checklists feel safe and predictable, while feelings are unpredictable, and I didn't need more unpredictability.

Not wanting to assume importance while also wanting to help, I asked, "Would you like me to write a eulogy for the rosary?" "Yes, your Abuelita would love that," my mom said as she was cleaning her drugstore reading glasses.

The house was filled with the familiar morning smells of growing up: My dad's cologne, greasy bacon, and dark coffee. Sitting at the kitchen table with my mom, where my Abuelita had sung happy birthday to me so many times before, I knew it was real, but I kept it from sinking in. She had died, and now I was writing her eulogy.

I wanted to show up for my Abuelita how she had shown up in her own life: strong and dignified.

On Thursday, April 28, 2022, Ana Maria Barrera, beloved great-grandmother, grandmother, and mother, passed away peacefully and gracefully at 87. Ana Maria was born on May 31, 1934, in Linares, Nuevo Leon, Mexico, to Jose Rodriguez and Ercilia Mendoza. On April 23, 1955, she married Emerico Barrera. She and her husband immigrated from Mexico to the US in 1962 with three children. They raised two daughters,

Cati and Nellie, and two sons, Pepe and Emerico Jr.
Affectionately known as 'Welita' to her grandchildren,
she spent her life working hard and being creative. She
was driven to make a better life for her family.

As I wrote, I kept coming back to the knowing that
she loved me well, and I loved her well. She was with
me during every milestone—ballet dance recitals,
high school graduation, college graduation, when
I got married—and all along the way, predictably
whispering to me how friendships were so meaningful, how dancing was so fun, how earrings finish off
a look, and how much she loved me and prayed for
me. As a child, we'd go to the pulga, the flea market,
and set up a booth to sell trinkets on the weekends.
I loved being with her; I loved how proud she was
of me. She taught me how to honor my parents and
God and work hard. She was remarkable, constantly
creating something out of nothing and loving
us well.

I marveled at her as I wrote. She significantly impacted
my life, yet she had not been a socialite or held an
outwardly visible job. She did not dress to impress or
seek to amass. She was unremarkable by pop culture
standards and yet entirely remarkable to me.

Ana Maria (Anita) was most in her joy when dancing

with her husband, Emerico. Anita and Emerico danced their way through 50 years of marriage. She was proficient at helping things grow, especially her family and her garden. She found community in her church, prayer group, and the baile. She was known for her strong spirit, quick wit, and devotion to God. Her grandchildren remember their Welita for her unwavering love, open arms, and handmade tortillas.

Writing her eulogy left me with big, big questions: *What if achievement and power aren't requisites for a good life? What if a well-lived life has more to do with being loved and loving well?*

I saw my mother moving through the hallways of the house I grew up in, and I felt myself doing the same. I could feel the spirit of my Abuelita, and I thought of my daughters. Somehow, we all mingled inside my heart. It is as if a long, invisible thread wove through us, connecting our tears and joys across the generations. But something more than that, too. I could not put words to it—it was simply a feeling that was neither joy nor sadness but presence. Maybe love.

Carl Jung elegantly expressed the idea that, "Every woman extends backward into her mother and forward into her daughter."

I believe this is true in every way—physically, spiritually, mentally, and beyond.

It blew my mind when I learned that female babies are born with all the eggs they will ever carry. This means that when my Abuelita carried my mother inside her womb, my mother held the beginnings of me, just as I have always held the beginnings of my two daughters. They now hold a piece of any children they may ever have. Part of me was there when Abuelita was abused, part of me was there when she made a life in Mexico, and part was there when she became a mother to my mom.

My Abuelita and mom's bodies were my first physical homes, and my spirit was born of theirs. There are both intergenerational traumas and intergenerational strengths. I am because they are; as I heal and step into my power and wholeness, I find they are because I am.

This is the way of women. As daughters and mothers, we move and experience in visible ways individually but also in invisible ways together. We carry each other's pains, joys, confidences, and insecurities. We carry each other, physically and spiritually, from beginning to end. We are alive in the *gentle return* to where we come from and who we have always been. Both brand new and ancient, all at once.

I barely remember delivering the eulogy aloud, but I will always remember my Abuelita.

I love you, Welita. You are always with me.

Te quiero mucho, Welita.

Siempre estaremos juntas.

Lend me your hope for a while,
a time will come when I will heal,
and I will lend my renewed hope to others.
—Eloise Cole

TRAUMA *of* CHILDBIRTH

As women, while we may feel alone in this world, in truth, we are never alone. We are always sitting with each other, in person or in spirit, our hearts sewn together by experience and song across distances and generations, a magical sisterhood of power and possibility. I know this because I have lived it and continue to live it. Let me tell you a story about being born.

It is January 18, 2017, and I'm checking into the hospital. Baby #2 is on her way. I know something is different this time, but I can't explain what. I push the thoughts to the back of my mind, where they can get lost in the fog with the undone to-do lists. No one will know.

During labor for baby #1, the nurse told me, "Each baby has their way of getting here." She said women will have an easier time if they don't clutch to their expectations for dear life. I tried to take her advice.

I meet my labor and delivery nurse, Sarah, around 7:30 p.m. She walks in, professional and kind. "What kind of labor are you hoping for?" I explain that I want minimally invasive labor. "During my first labor, I staked my pride on not having an epidural— but I'm wiser now." This time, I labor without meds for two hours, get an epidural, labor for two more hours, and push for FOUR minutes. Lightning fast compared to my first labor.

At 12:53 a.m., I hear a big cry. A healthy baby girl! She is here. But she is shades of blue and purple. "Where is she going?" I ask.

"She sucked in a lot of amniotic fluid. We have to help her," a voice says.

The baby is being cared for, but the doctor and nurses realize my placenta is not coming out. Thoughts race through my mind. What do you mean by *not coming out*? I have just given birth, I haven't held my baby yet, and now I am more in the unknown. My eyes dart around, looking for reassurance. It doesn't come.

Blood is spilling out of me and onto the black tarp on

the floor. I am not an expert, but I know this wasn't how the first labor and delivery went. "Ma'am, we're going to try a few things to get your placenta out—but if that doesn't work, we'll have to do a C-section. In a few minutes, we'll wheel you to the O.R."

"Okay," I say. *Every baby has a unique way of coming into the world*, pulses through my mind. I am losing blood, and my placenta needs to come out.

Sometime after I deliver my daughter and before I am wheeled to the operating room, I bring God close. I have to. I start to hum.

There is power in the name of Jesus
There is power in the name of Jesus
There is power in the name of Jesus
To break every chain, break every chain, break every chain
To break every chain, break every chain, break every chain

As they roll me out of the delivery room, I lock eyes with my bearded husband and tell him I love him and that I will be okay. One is the truth, and one I hope is the truth. My daughter, Luciana, is minutes old, and I haven't even seen her face. No matter; I have to go.

As they lift my body from the bed to the gurney, I hum.
As they wheel me into the operating room, I hum.
As they take off my bra—just in case—I hum.
As they strap my legs to stirrups, I hum.
As they connect I.V.s to my arms, I hum.

In the O.R., I am surrounded by strangers. Sarah was the only person's name I knew. And even though I had only interacted with Sarah for four hours prior, she had seen me go from casual to excruciating labor pain. Sarah had seen me and helped me push a human being out of my body, and Sarah had seen things take a turn for the worse.

I lay helpless on the operating table, seeing brighter-than-bright fluorescent lights, a large digital clock with red numbers, a symphony of nurses, and feeling blasts of cold air.

My body starts to convulse. The nurses scurry to find as many white cotton blankets as possible to weigh my body down and keep me steady. It feels like someone has unzipped my skin, and the insides of my body are exposed to the icy temperature of the operating room. I feel like a dead deer being skinned and quartered.

While pinned down by the blankets, convulsing and

staring at the flecked acoustic ceiling tiles, the doctor sticks her entire forearm into me and roots around for my placenta. "It's stuck. We'll have to try something else." *Something else?* She reaches for a serrated spoon, inserts it into me, and starts to scrape. "This will cause fertility issues later. If this doesn't work, we'll get the hose."

With every turn of her wrist, she scrapes quarter-sized bits and pieces of my body onto her sterile silver tray.

The only part of my body I have control over is my neck, so I tilt it toward Sarah and say, "I'm losing blood. I can feel it." And then I continue humming.

There is power in the name of Jesus
There is power in the name of Jesus

"Yes, you are losing blood, but more blood is coming," Sarah confirms. Minutes later, the doctor yells, "Where's the blood?"

"We have someone at the door waiting for the blood—it'll be right up." My vision starts to go grey, and I can feel my faculties shutting down. *Nope, no more energy for that. Or that. Or that.* For as long as I have the energy, I hum.

There is power in the name of Jesus

And then I stop humming because I just can't anymore. "What song are you humming?" Sarah leans in and asks. "A church song," I mumble. She takes over humming for me. I can feel her hand in mine, giving me warmth. I don't have the energy to hum with her, but I can hear the hymn, and amid the chaos, I feel peaceful. And then I close my eyes.

The doctors give me a blood transfusion, scrape out my placenta, and take me back to my original room.

I begin convulsing in shock. My body shakes and trembles—teeth chattering incessantly. Desperate for water, I ask, "can . . . I . . . have . . . water . . . please?" But I'm not allowed water. They bring me a pink plastic jar full of ice chips as consolation.

For three hours, I stare at the mirror, convulse, and robotically eat through the ice chips, my mind sinking deeper and deeper into a heavy and still abyss. As I hit the bottom of the pitcher of ice chips, they roll my newborn baby into the room. "She's hungry," says a nurse. "Yes, of course, bring her to me." And just like that, I went into mom mode. The mode where we do what is needed, whatever that is. The mode where love takes over, whatever the cost. The mom mode that is sewn deeply into our DNA.

Because mothering is so beautiful and lauded, no one sees that some good mothers are alive but not living. Their essence is being scraped from the inside out and offered as a sacrifice on the altar of motherhood. If we're not careful, we can spend our entire lives in mom mode, only oriented to what children need and never giving time, space, or consideration to what we need.

The next day, the doctors explain that I hemorrhaged 50% of my blood. "We're glad we had her blood type."

I know something is different than before—but I don't know how to explain it.

Five years have passed, and I'm walking that same blue and purple baby down the hallway for her first day of kindergarten. "One last huggie and kissie?" Luciana asks me. "Always, baby."

I hop back in the car and pop on a podcast, needing a minute to lick my wounds on her first day of school, when I hear, "Of course, the trauma of childbirth." Teachers and wisdom are flying around us—like butterflies in a garden, offering their beauty if only we can be present enough to see it or hear it, like a podcast.

I have never heard someone say trauma and child-birth in the same sentence. Or maybe I have, and I wasn't ready to acknowledge it. Our bodies and physiology are so compassionate in that way, protecting us until we can hold it. And suddenly, it was all there—neatly packed in the back of my mind and ready to be looked at. *You lost a lot of blood. We're taking you to the O.R.* Memories of how my body was scraped from the inside and how my vagina became an entry point for the doctor's tools and forearm—utilitarian. *You'll probably have PTSD. Here's a prescription for antide-pressants. You could hemorrhage for two weeks after, so watch for bleeding.* The wounds and the trauma of childbirth keep flying through my thoughts. It was a physical and emotional injury. It was complex. And instead of seeking help, in delusion, maybe denial and avoidance, I poured myself into my family.

After so many years, I dare to think *maybe it was trau-matizing*. And I start to soften into the notion that I experienced trauma. That part of me that was pro-tecting me, holding the un-bare-able and unbearable, is tired—it is time to set it down.

I ask Anthony if he has pictures of Luciana's birth. He hands me his phone. "Oh, I've never seen these," I share as I swipe through the images. *How could I not have seen the pictures of the day I brought this baby into the world?* I'm flipping through the photos, seeing the nurses handling my six-pound baby, my head turned in her direction and facial expression very clearly communicating I want my baby. Each picture is grainy and brown, full of beauty and deep seriousness. With the scanning of each photo, I feel my heart swelling and the tears forming. I'm being transported to that operating room, to the fear, the helplessness, and the gratitude for surviving.

When women are at our most powerful, we are integrated and whole. We show up with equal parts mind, body, and soul. But that's hard and rare. Most women are disintegrated—cutting off parts of themselves because they are too painful to bare or to bear.

I start to have deep compassion for myself, for all I had been through and all I had tucked away. And then, that compassion extended outward. Over a café lunch, I ask my mom about her birthing experiences. And as she shared my birth story, my heart broke for her.

"I remember the drive. I blankly stared out the car window, asking God to give me strength. What else could I do? I had no idea what was going to occur. I was put in a room with other laboring women. The only thing between me and their primal screams was a cheap hospital curtain. No one except for nurses, doctors, and laboring women was allowed in the room. I didn't have my mom or your dad; I was alone. I bit into a towel and tried to deal with the pain, pushing you out with all my might. I still remember the awful sensation of vomiting from the medicine."

The hard truth that she had no one to walk alongside her through her pain devastated me. Soon, that compassion extended even further. We, as women, bring life into the world, and it can be traumatic; we can go through a lot. How many of us are walking around in pain, alone, shifting into mom mode because that's what is necessary? How many of us cut off parts of who we are because what's the use?

Who can sit in compassion and hold space for us while we figure it out and heal?

Women can.

It's not that we need to be fixed. It's that we need to be heard. We need the dignity of one another's attention as we share what we have experienced to unravel the feelings and memories we hold inside. One of the greatest gifts my friendships with women have given me is a warm embrace, and I've been through that, too. Whenever I have shared my story or listened intently to a friend's story, my heart has been sewn together with theirs. Somehow, that connection helps me stand taller and feel less alone, like I am a part of something great, a magical sisterhood brimming with power and possibility.

Unconsciously, I have surrounded myself with women who have been able to help me through. Therapists, doctors, professors, colleagues, classmates, friends, cousins, and readers. Each woman holding space for me, not rushing to change me or to give me solutions, only saying, *Tell me more. That's understandable.* And, *I've been through that too.* Their empathy has helped me accept my truth and move on.

It can be difficult and uncomfortable to sit with someone and hear their voice crack, see their eyes well up, and witness flashes of helplessness. Hearing such harrowing stories can bring up so much that the listener hasn't tended to. Listening to a girlfriend, a sister, or a mother is a gift. Giving our attention and presence cannot be wrapped or quantified, but it is felt and heals.

Along the way, I have shared parts of Luciana's birth story with women I trust, and, conversation by conversation, the insides that were scraped out of me were stitched back together in love.

I know that women may present as schoolteachers, photographers, or engineers, but there's much more to us than that. I know our depth and dimensions. I know the wells of strength, compassion, and power inside us.

When we can be brave enough to listen to one another, share, and ask each other hard questions—when we can surrender our urge to put a glossy sheen over our experiences and move straight to meaningful connections—we become stronger. We can sit with each other as we learn how to bear our own stories; rather than bearing our hurts, we begin our *gentle return*.

As it turns out, now is the moment
you have been waiting for.
—Lucinda Williams

MOM

I dial the phone number I've known all my life, and my dad picks up. "Hi, Dad."

"Happy Mother's Day, Catia," he remarks. His tone of voice somehow always hides a smirk. I pause. "Oh, yes. Thank you."

"What? Is that weird?"

"I just didn't expect it." I'm a mom, but I still consider myself a daughter.

It's May 2019, and I am a mother of two young girls. But a big part of me—hopefully, a forever part of me—identifies as a daughter, his daughter. This is a foolish statement in middle age, but I cling to it. "Is Mom there?"

"No, she went to go pick up your Abuelita."

In her 60s, my mom still identifies as a daughter, too. I call back a few hours later. My dad picks up the phone and calls my mom from the patio. "Nellie, it's Catia."

"Hi, Precious." My mom has called me Precious my whole life, reserving my middle name, Celeste, for when she's clenching her teeth in frustration.

"Hi, Mom. Happy Mother's Day," I say between quiet sobs, my chest filling with shallow puffs of air. I am living in Panama. The Central American country is two plane rides away from my childhood home, and I am unable to be with my mom on Mother's Day. And my heart aches. Without asking any questions, she replies, "I miss you, too."

"I miss you, Mom."

"We'll see each other in June," she reassures me, trying to soothe my pain. "I know," I mumble, knowing she's right but not liking that June is a whole month away.

I start to cry but hold back my tears, trying to have a decent conversation. Pointless. Then she passes the phone to my Abuelita, my grandmother, whom I lovingly call Welita, and I start crying again.

"Feliz Día de las Madres. La amo." In Spanish, she tells me to close my eyes and feel her hugging me. "Feel my big hug full of love." She repeats this over and over. When Welita starts weeping, we say we love each other, hang up, and I explode into tears.

When I was younger, I thought my dad hung the moon. He's handsome, photogenic, and powerful. He was at the helm of our family and the family business. He helped me with math homework. He taught me how to write. "Write what you know, Catia. Try again; go back and tie the end to the beginning." His approval meant almost everything to me. When I was a little girl, the light shone brightly on my dad. Business partners gave him the power seat at the dinner table. He was involved in our community, and people smiled when he entered the room. The admiration I had for my dad ran deep.

My mom was great, too. She immigrated from Mexico to the U.S. with her family when she was six. As a child, her entire family would pile into the bed of a truck, with only a tarp to protect them from the elements and drive from the southernmost tip of Texas to Wisconsin to pick beets and cucumbers. They lived in a one-bedroom house with dirt floors. While her parents worked in the fields, as a six-year-old, my mom would care for her infant brother. As a teenager, she would go to school, and after school, she would clock in at the local grocery store, working until 11 p.m. most nights. She graduated high school and attended a two-year fashion school in North Texas. Spanish was her first language, yet she was studying higher education—in English!

On June 12, 1983, my parents were married at the ages of 24 and 25. Because it was the middle of tomato season—a crop my dad helped his dad harvest—my parents didn't go on a honeymoon. They were married on a Saturday, and both returned to work the following Monday.

Soon after, with the support of their families, my mom and dad started their own beer corner stores called *Pop-A-Top*. Eventually, these corner stores morphed into *Holiday Wine and Liquor*. Today, my folks have been in business for 41 years, own ten stores, and have employed and created opportunities for thousands of families.

My mom went from being an immigrant to a migrant worker who slept in a one-bedroom house with dirt floors to becoming a real estate investor and the owner of a multimillion-dollar retail company while loving her husband and children well. But I never saw any of that. I saw my mom as meek.

She didn't do anything I associated with power or prestige. She did not dress in designer wear; she did not wear makeup and was somewhat in the shadows. I loved her, but my mom was not my hero when I was a little girl. My dad was my hero. During my adolescence, I felt some tension with my mom, like I had gotten the memo on how to be powerful, and she hadn't.

The way I viewed my mom changed the moment I became a mother.

I suddenly needed my mother like I had never needed her before. I needed her comfort, her wisdom, and her hugs. I needed her to teach me how to mother. I needed her to tell me it was going to be okay. And that crack in my arrogance began a lovely, deep, kind, gratitude-filled relationship with her.

When I became a mother, my eyes opened. I realized my idea of her was more like a caricature that artists draw on busy streets in tourist cities. My picture of her resembled her, but it needed a more complete, in-depth, and accurate portrayal of her. I mainly had seen her as my mom, but not as a whole woman.

When I became a mom, I became aware of all my mom did and how she supported and sacrificed for us. I appreciated how smart she is and how she always gives me good advice. I began to realize that many of her circumstances were choices and that she is living her life the way she wants. My appreciation and admiration have only gone up every day after that initial realization.

On this Mother's Day, I am exploding into tears because I know how important she is, how sweet this season of our life is, and how well she has loved and mothered me. I'm no longer the bratty young girl who thinks she knows more than her mom. I sit at her feet and watch and learn, in awe of how hard she has worked and how well she raised me. Raising a daughter who feels well-loved is how the world changes and my mom did her part.

I cry because I know there aren't many more Mother's Days we will celebrate together. I know that life ends, and I'm doing all I can to soak up every moment with my mom and show her—albeit awkwardly—how much I value, admire, and appreciate her.

Blaming is futile, but I'll do it anyway. I blame patriarchy for teaching me that there was only one way: convincing me that power was loud and austere and weakness closer to quiet and supple. I blame patriarchy for pedestalizing all things masculine and sneering at all things feminine. I blame patriarchal ideas for causing me to split from my mother and her essence. For so long, I was a young woman trying to live the way patriarchy wanted me to—with masculine values, forsaking my feminine. Always falling short, constantly feeling incomplete, and always judging my performance. The hero's journey is not the heroine's journey.

When I became a mother, I was suddenly privy to an entirely new reality where I could nurture, be, and connect. It's not about competing; it is about connecting. That entry into motherhood was a gift of insight into who my mother was and is and all her glory.

For the last eight years, as I stepped into motherhood, I began to realize what I had, and my mom and I have grown closer and closer. We have each revealed tender parts of ourselves, walking with each other through life-altering hurts and holding each other's hands when words aren't enough.

I remember one stretch of time that began as a practicality but ended up deepening my understanding of myself and divine femininity.

In 2022, when Anthony began to work out of town, my mom offered to come to help me. I jumped at the chance. Once you're married with kids, the times are few and far between when you're with your mother for extended periods. I was glad to have her but also felt guilty for not being able to host her. "Mom, are you sure you want to come? I will be busy with school and work and won't be able to hang out."

She assures me she'll be okay and knows she is coming to help and not to be hosted. She agrees to visit once a month while my husband was commuting during the work week. Once a month, she helps me make breakfast, pack school lunches, and comb high ponytails. We are a house full of women with no men to tend to. It's glorious.

The days are filled with hugs, tears, emotional swings, and much love. We cry over bacon and breakfast as I ask her about life without her mother. My questions about Welita walk us through a vault where we feel the sanctity of the relationships between the woman who raised her, her, and the women I am raising. I sit there, knowing I'm on hallowed ground.

The girls are in bed tonight. I'm fresh out of the shower and decide to check in on my mom. I walk into her room to review the next day's agenda. Her barely open eyes give away what her voice and heart won't—she's tired and needs rest. But she's a mom, my mom, and rest doesn't come easy.

"Do you need any help," she asks as she sits in bed.

"No thanks, Mom. But can I get you anything?" We joke that I am tucking her into bed and turning off her bedside lamp like a child.

"Goodnight, Mom. I love you."

"I love you, Precious."

I gently close the door and feel my heart swell and ache. The moment feels incomplete. The notion that my mom, my mom, is here right now sinks into my belly. This woman is here. I stand in the hallway, remembering when she told me that as a new mom, she cherished the times I would get up in the middle of the night because it was her special alone time with me; she didn't have to share me with anyone. *Go back in*, I think, *hug her, kiss her*. I take two seconds to catch my breath. That 'goodnight' just wasn't enough. I open her bedroom door.

"Mom?"
"Yes, Precious?"

"I came to kiss you."

I lean into her fine hair and kiss her forehead. I lay my head on her head and breathe her in, expressing my love and hoping she receives it. The moment is deliciously thick, almost too much, like a large spoonful of peanut butter.

In moments like this, I am trying to make up for the lost time, trying to heal what was split for decades. It's not about NOT loving my dad or my dad not being my hero—because he is. But so is my mom. I have two heroes. I see all that her divine feminine has brought to the table of my life. I am immeasurably better for it.

Sometimes, when I hug her, I find myself wanting to sink deeper into her, close the gap, and then realize it's not a physical gap I want to close but an emotional one.

Tonight, I pull my head away from hers, grateful I chose to walk back into her room.

"Goodnight, Mom. I love you."

"I love you too. God bless you," she answers back. I shut her door gently. That was it—a *gentle return*. Now we are complete.

Everybody loves freedom.
—Alexandra Grace Holm

AGGRIEVED

Luciana, a newly minted three-year-old in 2020, came to our bedroom in the middle of the night. I awoke and made out her silhouette. "Daddy," she said in her sweet, young voice. "Yes, baby," Anthony answered. She toddled over, folded over the corner of our bed, propped herself up, and crawled over the knotted blankets to cuddle. She was like a living puzzle piece, finding her place between Anthony and me in the dark of night. She tossed and turned and let out three-year-old yawns. Just as her eyes were getting heavy, she reached over to Anthony and asked, "Daddy, hold my hand?"

I contracted, and my thoughts raced—*don't bother him. He's sleeping. You're already in our bed. We're already awake. What more could you want?* I held my tongue, and not a second-and-a-half later, Anthony whispered, "Always."

He gave her his right index finger. Her left hand curled around his finger as she brought it close to her rising and falling chest. I turned over, heartbroken for myself and relieved for my daughter. Patriarchy is hell to root out.

From a young age, girls are taught not to be too much.

Don't desire constant attention.
Don't ask too many questions.
Don't jump off the furniture.
Don't wear loud clothes.
Don't be too much.
Don't be assertive.
Don't be too thin.
Don't be sexual.
Don't be loud.
Don't be ugly.
Don't be fat.

Do speak.
Do be thin.
Do be beautiful.
Do make money.
Do ask questions.
Do martyr yourself.
Do get good grades.
Do wear cute clothes.

Do have fun and play.
Do tell me what you want.
Do want me to pay attention to you.
Do comb your hair like everyone else.

Just don't do any of that too much, either.

Be medium.
Be agreeable.
Maddening patriarchal expectations.

We girls are so young when we start absorbing these messages that we don't know to question them. Fish don't know they're in water. And adults, already brainwashed and steeped in unspoken, unwritten cultural expectations, keep us caged along the way until we become young women.

We come into the world big, loud, and free. And, over time, we get our edges trimmed, muted, and discouraged. The too-little parts of us get cheered on just enough to get us to the middle ground—and the too-much parts get squashed and suffocated just enough to get us to the middle ground.

In our youth, we are taught to prize the divine masculine qualities of assertiveness, risk-taking, order, objectivity, and subliminally, even the toxic masculine qualities of control, aggression, and hostility to femininity. Simultaneously, we are taught to look down upon the divine feminine qualities of intuition, worth, sensuality, and expression. We're taught to prize things outside of who we are and, sometimes, outside of who our mothers are. And because of these unseen and tsunami-like forces, our spirits split in two, creating a canyon.

Because of the split, as a young girl, the *moniker* a guy's girl was a badge of honor for me. I didn't want to be a regular girl; regular girls were too fussy. Girls were weak. Being like a girl was insulting to me. I would have been closer to my mom if not for the split. I would not have overlooked her choice for a quieter domestic life for my dad's more visible life. I would have revered her devotion to us, her thoughtfulness, and her strength instead of taking it for granted. Things would have been different had I not been steeped in patriarchal beliefs, had it not been for the split.

As young women, we are deemed *acceptable* after our individuality is stripped away—after our too-little and too-much parts get fixed.

When we don't ruffle any feathers and when we don't make people uncomfortable, everyone applauds.

We may want to say no. We may want to hold boundaries. We may want to have the last piece of pizza. Still, we don't because we have been brainwashed to believe that we can live and enjoy ourselves only as long as it's not inconvenient for anyone else.

In my mid-twenties, a casual acquaintance asked me to go out of town with him to see a concert, and I instantly knew I didn't want to go. But instead of saying, "no, thank you," I spent a weekend with my stomach in knots, agonizing over the decision. I was so nervous to say, "No, thank you," that I had to write my reasoning on index cards when I called him. Instead, I would have absorbed his potential discomfort rather than possibly have him feel it.

Initially, these expectations feel unreasonable because young girls are wise and strong and know what feels good, and martyrdom, suppression, and living in shadows don't feel good. But we look to the women around us, to the television, to the culture—and we see women giving beyond the point of comfort, sometimes giving to their detriment. And so, as young girls, we eventually fall in line. Like horses being broken, we know we are here to serve.

We know it doesn't feel good—that we don't want it—but we do it, partly because all the good women around us are doing it and partly because we are convinced that this is how to be seen, validated, and applauded.

We are vying for the spot of *the most sacrificial woman*.

At least we can win at losing.

We think that if we ignore ourselves enough, someone will notice us.

But no one ever does.

Eventually, a good girl steps into the role of a good woman. Our invisible badge of honor shows everyone that we followed all the rules and are marked safe. Our dwelling is built somewhere in the middle.

We stay put because we know our badge will be revoked if we step out of the middle. We will no longer be looked upon as a good woman. We will be labeled selfish, high maintenance, or too much. I did not escape these messages.

I am lucky that the men in my life are loving and kind. My dad, husband, brothers, mentors, and a handful of friends have always been stand-up men and have loved me well. But for sure, unconscious patriarchal beliefs have affected our dynamics.

Things would have been different had I not been steeped in patriarchal beliefs, had it not been for the split.

My daughters, Alexandra and Luciana, favor their father in many ways. They love him, cling to him, and seek him out. Their dad works in big buildings downtown. Their dad pays for dinner. Their dad is a commodity, and I'm always around. Sometimes, when Anthony thinks the scales are tipped, he'll say, "Your mama is so awesome!" And I'm always appreciative when he does that. But the truth is my girls think their dad hung the moon. And I understand them because, at one point, I was them.

But I was the first voice they heard; it was my heartbeat lulling them into peace. Then, when they were born, I devoted myself to nursing and nourishing them, using my body to feed their bodies. I live within every part of them, and they live within every part of me. I am their home base. I also hung the moon; they may not know it yet, but they will one day.

Patriarchy's effects on my life are complicated and nuanced, and I'm aggrieved.

We pay a price for staying in the middle. Some of us

lose our fire, some of our sparks fall dim, and some of our souls wither away. Some of us erupt. We get so tired of being suppressed—all those years of over-looking, giving, sacrificing, and performing—that we crack and explode.

What looks like a mental breakdown is really a reckoning, a rearranging of what always should have been.

I thought a woman's power was somewhere over yonder and that once I arrived, legitimacy and worthiness would be bestowed upon me in a crowning achievement, and everything would fall into place. Only, I never arrived because striving from within a cage is not striving at all. I was serving an invisible master outside of myself, reaching for a prize my heart of hearts did not love or desire. I was living through a lens that was not mine, a masculine lens that never fit me quite right. I was constantly falling short of living in my power because I was living out a version of power that was not mine when, all along, I could have been creating my own.

My life has been steeped in these messages of patriarchy. I have long felt patriarchy's shadow on the shoreline of my soul. I have heard it professing to protect when it actually precludes and prevents—seen it standing guard around my heart like a cage.

I am a *good woman*, as it were. I am kind and polite and absorb other people's discomfort. I am not confrontational. I still take the high road and usually defer to my husband. But where these qualities were once formed in fear by the bars of patriarchy, I am finding new sources of power within them through a *gentle return* to myself and my essence.

And this is the struggle. As women, we must find and affirm the power within ourselves even as we live within the long shadow of patriarchy.

We must step out of the cage that is the middle, beyond the shadow, and into our light. We must learn to live in our inner knowing, and we must teach our girls even as we teach ourselves, especially as we teach ourselves, that we are not too much or too little when we are ourselves.

We must turn and choose a *gentle return* to the power at our feminine centers, where we can find pleasure, fulfillment, worth, and satisfaction by standing in the truth of who we are. And we must stand here, as women, together.

At our best, when our divine masculine and divine feminine are singing, we don't feel obligated to fall in line, we don't go along to get along, and we don't forsake ourselves for others. When we live in our full power, embracing both the masculine and the feminine, our strength and sensitivity, we don't look outside of ourselves to find someone to save us or someone to blame. When we are attuned to our inner knowing, we know that people will be there to love and support us and that we, as women, get to define our lives.

When dancing through life and embodying our power, women move in integrity, our highest selves, embracing all our parts, knowing they were never too little or too much.

When we are in our power, we honor our inner knowing,
even if it's inconvenient,
even when we need to step out of the middle.

To create one's own life takes courage.
—Georgia O'Keefe

MISTY

Every woman must choose: will she go along to get along, or will she risk her reputation and choose to stop? We must choose, not just once, but every day, over and over. The older I get, the less I care about going along or getting along. And the older I get, the more I choose myself.

I am unsure what the world expects of you on your birthday, but it's not melancholy. Questions run like ticker tape through my mind. *Will people see me? Do I matter? Do they know me enough to celebrate me well? Will the day match my expectations?* These internal questions weigh me down. The quality of our lives equals the quality of our thoughts. We can live the same life and be grateful one day and pissed another.

On my 39th birthday—as much as I was excited about turning 39—I was not enthusiastic about the actual day. On birthdays, I walk around with a level of impossible tension. I want to be happy, but most things seem to disappoint. I've been able to hold it together in recent years, but most years, I cry with no one or nothing to blame; it's just a weird swirling of unidentifiable emotions. Recently, I found an old card from a college boyfriend that was once attached to a bouquet of flowers. The card read, "I hope these make your day better." My birthday affliction has been with me for a while.

To negate this seemingly inevitable melancholy, I have learned to become directive. Maybe if I get each piece just right, the details will magically come together. Decadent buttercream cake. Bunches of brightly colored balloons. Fragrant flowers. And for my 39th birthday, I asked for a specific present—horse riding lessons. I knew I'd ride valiantly like Robin Wright in "Wonder Woman" if I could ride horseback.

For the first few lessons, I rode a mare named Arrow. But really, Arrow let me ride her. Arrow's light brown mane glistened in the sun. I was such a novice that sometimes she would nod off. I was happy to be with her, taking in the view and feeling the majesty of a horse. A few lessons in, just when I was getting used to her, the horse trainer switched up the horses and suggested that I ride Misty—another mare—instead. I thought nothing of it until a young girl named Lindsey, no older than 15, offered to go with me to get Misty from her paddock. "She's tough," the young lady said. "She's moody; you just have to be firm with her." I started to perk up. I was a beginner, and if I couldn't handle getting her from her paddock alone, how would I be able to ride her?

We walked through the musty barn, our riding boots crunching dry hay and kicking up powdery dirt. When we stopped at the entrance of Misty's paddock, there were three horses. I knew which one Misty was because she took a few steps back. Lindsey approached with the lead, and Misty stiffened her body and neck in disapproval. When the worn purple lead was clipped to her halter, Misty whipped her tail side to side in frustration. I caught some horsehair across my cheek. My first horse injury.

Lindsey asked if I wanted her to walk Misty to the stable, and I said yes. I was a little scared. Unlike Arrow, who was strong but gentle, Misty was strong and vocal. As I started to tack up Misty, my horse trainer joined me. "Now, Misty can be cantankerous and very particular." I had just heard two people dig into Misty in less than 10 minutes, so I was curious: *What was the negativity around Misty?*

As I brushed her out, I stared into her eyes, trying to connect, get underneath her mood, and go deeper. Her muscles were tense, and her dark brown eyes were pools of welled-up emotion. *Oh, I know this. I've been here before.* My fear went away as I brushed her hair and tacked her up. "Be careful with the girth; she startles when it's tightened." *Understandable.* "Gentle. Got it."

On our way to the arena, I thought *Misty is defensive because she is protecting herself. I've been there.* As women, we are often hurt, abused, belittled, and taken advantage of. Our history teaches us to be wary and, sometimes, defensive. We get support and heal if we are lucky, but some of us aren't so lucky. Some of us are forced to walk around life with open wounds just trying to get the grocery shopping taken care of.

Before I mounted her, I looked at Misty and thanked her. "I'm here to listen and learn from you; I'm your student." She made me prove it. We warmed up and trotted, and with every exercise, I'd check in with her. "Hi, Misty, I'm listening." I knew her defensive and skeptical parts because as much as I present like Arrow—strong, gentle, and easygoing—sometimes, I want to be like Misty—vocal and unwavering. The horse trainer kept making excuses and apologizing for Misty's temperament. I finally said, "just because she doesn't want to listen to me, doesn't mean she's moody. It just means she doesn't want to listen to me." I wasn't talking about horses anymore. Riding Misty and connecting with her was a portal to something broader—women who are tired of going along to get along.

There are legions of us who are gold medalists at going along to get along. We are artful, good at finessing the situation, doing it just this time, and swallowing it—all while we seethe and rot from the inside out. We can be Princess Kate—applauded and upheld, or Meghan Markle—denigrated and cut down. Either way, women pay the price. And when women are cut down, it signals to the rest of us: behave, or else you're next. The less vocal pay a price of internal disconnection, and the more vocal—the Mistys—pay a price of external disconnection.

During the lesson, I melted into her. I wanted Misty to know it wasn't her fault. I wanted her to see that she wasn't bad or difficult or too much and that she deserved a voice and deserved to be heard. That riding lesson should have been about my technique, achieving a rising trot, and getting closer to Robin Wright "Wonder Woman" status, but it wasn't. It was about validating Misty and standing in solidarity with her and all women mischaracterized as difficult, cantankerous, or moody.

Culture conditions us to feel small and beholden. We have been convinced that our preferences could be more convenient and cause problems. We've been shown that if we go along, we may lose our sense of self, but we will get to belong. And we have been shown that if we don't go along, we may keep our sense of self, but we will be ostracized. Women are shamed into always being pleasant and easygoing.

We, too, bristle when the lead is brought to our paddock. We shake our tails at those who wish to control us. We look for the ones who will see us for who we are and tell us loudly, "Just because you don't want to listen doesn't mean you're moody; it just means you are yourself." And then, when we are truly ready to step out of the harness of society's expectations, we must tell ourselves that very message. And that is what Misty invited me to do. I saw my own eyes in her eyes, and in her movement, my movement.

This is the choice that every woman must make: go along to get along or choose herself. This is a true birthday—a day when I choose myself.

On the other side of spiritual aridity is the space and language to claim the true nature of our souls. Because throwing off the unwanted saddle is not the end but rather the beginning, we must not only wrestle free of society's expectations but also get free of simply reacting to or rejecting them. We must get to the place beyond both, where we are free to look down at our hands, our hearts, our bodies, and our souls, and truly see ourselves, then truly connect to ourselves. It's then that we truly choose for ourselves.

In that grace and that terrifying expanse of freedom is the invitation to a gentle return of our deepest feminine nature: to embrace our impulses, to run free in the windy fields of our lives, and to stand in our skin, whatever that means and however it looks for each of us.

May we all be inspired by Misty's courage. May we each know that we as women are not difficult; instead, we are ready to choose ourselves in our full dignity. This is the kind of birthday—the rebirth of choosing yourself—that I can celebrate every time.

Keep some room in your heart
for the unimaginable.
—Mary Oliver

———————————

LAS MUJERES INCREIBLES

There are always voices guiding us along our path if only we are quiet enough to listen.

For so long, gyms have been where I've found my people. Knowing this, I went out to find a gym a few days after arriving in Panama in 2018.

I found one just off a barely paved road in the middle of a mostly vacant strip center. I searched the schedule for something familiar. Zumba! Perfect. My instructor, Lloel, was exuberant. He was tan and had bulging muscles with perfectly gelled hair. A professional dancer at a nearby hotel, Lloel welcomed me to his class with open arms. For months, I Zumba-ed my heart. Occasionally, he couldn't make it, and class would get canceled. There aren't backup Zumba instructors in the sleepy beach towns of Panama. *Could I, maybe, teach the class? No. But maybe?*

My face contorted in anticipatory embarrassment. My toes tapped up and down with nervousness as I called the gym owner, Alena, and offered myself up. "I don't have any formal training, and I can't teach Zumba, but I do know my way around music and a gym," I said over the phone. "I'd love to teach a class or classes if you ever need." I mean, what did I have to lose? I was going to the gym anyway. I didn't need to fear judgment—everyone was a stranger to me in Central America. "I don't think so, but thank you," she said. I was awash in awkwardness.

A few weeks later, my phone rang late at night. It was Alena. "Are you still up for teaching? We need someone to cover the Zumba class tomorrow morning." *Zumba? Yikes.* In a split second, I thought of Tina Fey's advice shared in her memoir: say yes and figure it out after. "I'd love to," I answered.

Students caught wind that Lloel would be absent from class, so only one woman showed up for class— Marie. God bless Marie. "And one, two, three, turn, two, three. Don't be shy!" As I was shouting steps to Marie, my mind was yelling at me. *You cannot be a Zumba instructor. You have no idea what you are doing. This is mortifying.* I had nowhere to turn. I had nowhere to hide. I was stuck. I looked like and felt like a fool, and poor Marie had to watch as I set myself aflame with a combustible combination of trying, reaching, and humiliation.

THE WEIGHTS

I would never teach Zumba again. I did not ever want to teach Zumba again. So, I called the gym owner and said, "I'll teach weights and cardio."

"You start next week." Alena had only known me for a few weeks, but still, she gave me the keys to her business and trained me. "Cash only—place it in the bank bag. Sweep and mop after you are done. Turn off the air and lock up." My training took less time than it does to watch an episode of *Friends*.

On my first day of class, I realized I would be teaching in Spanish—a small oversight. Four women showed up: Andrea, Irina, Cynthia, and Lole. I made up entire routines on the spot with no actual plan. For some reason, they went along with it.

I didn't know any ladies before the class, but it was an absolute blast! I had only been in Panama for a few months and still didn't have friends. But I wanted friends. *Maybe they could be my friends?* Making friends isn't easy. There's so much risk and energy involved. And making friendships as mothers seems to be even more difficult. It requires more effort, coordination, and understanding.

THIS IS IT.

Anthony and I were slowing down, taking steps back from our careers, and enjoying our daughters more. The more we slowed down as a family, the more space our feelings had to surface. Feelings can be annoying for someone who is used to moving quickly through life.

For so long, I had been paying the meter on my career. Even when my career was running bars and restaurants, I felt like I had to be in constant forward motion. My worth was attached to who I was affiliated with, what I was producing, and what I could give others. I always had some impressive pieces to present. I had a great job at one of the most popular live music venues in Austin, where I interacted with famous people. I lived in a fancy neighborhood, published a book, and was a TEDx speaker. I could always hang my hat on some external thing—which always brought me relief. If they know this about me, then I will be validated.

But I started to notice at the end of every finish line,

I never felt any different. *Is this it?* My eyes darting around in curiosity. The thought would predictably ring through my head and my heart. Somehow, I always felt like the same person. I never felt better. I never felt more validated. I never felt more qualified. So, I began to get curious.

Who would I be without the hot poker of achievement moving me forward? Could I just be still?
Would I be happy with my life and myself if I was bare?

I decided to experiment. I decided to let it all go.

It helped that all the hooks I used to hang my hat on were nonexistent in Panama. There were no bookstores, no bloggers, and there was definitely no speaking circuit. Sometimes, there wasn't even electricity. No one was trying to amass a following or build a career. Immediately, it was a HUGE relief, like setting down a weighted bag. I never had to talk about work, my husband's job, or my career. None of it was necessary.

In the community where we landed, there was no competition, even subconsciously, for anything. And even though it took me time to find the language, my body and heart knew, *oh, this, this is it. This is what I've been needing.* And so, for the first time, maybe ever in my entire life, I was myself. I presented simply as Catia: mom of two girls, wife to a husband, a Mexican from Texas. That was it. I didn't have any stories attached to me.

When we let go of stories, we feel free.

My history wasn't important. The only thing that mattered was the present moment. The clothes I wore, the house I lived in, or the van I drove with its duct-taped bumper didn't matter. All that mattered was my friends and I went for coffee and bagels after gym class. Who I was married to didn't matter. All that mattered was that my husband was friendly.

And so, I would show up to my gym class and teach. I'd blare good music, cheer on my students, and laugh while I made up crazy workout combos.

There is a special kind of magic when people can be themselves and connect.

We started to schedule play dates, text back and forth, and share meals. My students had no idea this way of living was foreign to me. They, too, were just being themselves. I would cheer them on and say things like, "embarrassment doesn't exist here," and "no one gets left behind!" I'd remind them of how sexy and strong they were. We went from a teacher/student relationship to friend/friend.

Why hadn't I done this sooner? I had always found my people at a gym, so why hadn't I become an instructor sooner? Back at home, I had always coveted the idea of being a fitness instructor. It looked so exhilarating, so inspiring. But I never went for it because it wouldn't bring me accolades. It would detract from my more prominent and better goals. Being a fitness instructor would be fun, but it was unnecessary.

When striving for things on the exterior, it becomes easy to neglect our interior.

In Panama, I was away from it all. There was no greatness to be won. No one cared about goals or distinctions, so I didn't either. My gaze turned inward to fulfillment, and I felt my body and spirit shift. I was no longer antsy or seeking accomplishments. And eventually, I became content. My life was slow and simple and filled with meaningful relationships. I named our friend group "Las Mujeres Increibles." The Incredible Women.

Las Mujeres Increibles shared so many laughs, and we also had our tender moments. One day during class, Andrea started to cry. I stopped the class, walked over, and wrapped my arms around her. She kept crying on my shoulder, and I told her it would be okay and that she could cry. We stood in the middle of 10 women, hugging. When the tears stopped, we restarted the class—no explanation needed. A pause, some tears, and a bear hug were enough. It was so simple, and yet there was so much depth.

I taught three weekly classes, earning $20 per class, for about a year. My students and friends were from all over the world: Russia, South Africa, Panama, Slovakia, Peru, Chile, Brazil, Canada, the United States, Colombia, and Cuba. Distinct and yet connected. During my gym class, there was not one moment that I had to try to be *anything* to anyone. And neither did anyone else. During that hour, we could all just *be*. At the end of each week, I would take my full heart and my $60 in pay and go home fulfilled. Many a morning was spent with my friends, working out and physically pushing our bodies while giving ourselves time, as women, moms, and wives, to do self-care. It was the greatest surprise.

Getting to the point where we prioritize connection and joy can be difficult.

But in the *gentle return*, parts of us come alive that we didn't know existed.

IN THE END

Days before my family moved back to the U.S., the women in the class threw me a surprise farewell brunch. I was so tender and teary. As I walked into one of their homes and saw their new decorations, they yelled, "SURPRISE!" I wept. No one had ever thrown me a surprise party. All my girlfriends were there. I was overflowing with gratitude. The brunch layout was the best I'd ever seen, and every detail, from the infused water to the coffee cups, was perfect. I felt so loved and cared for. I was on the brink of tears the entire time, so when they presented me with the most touching and personal gifts, I let all the tears fall. I knew I had to tell them what I had realized.

I told them about landing in Panama and needing someone. I voiced how much I valued them. I told them how I was so grateful for their love and friendship, and I gave them the utmost thanks for guiding me back to myself. Me, without achievement. The real me. They showed me that I, on my own, was enough. I was enough. I'm not sure I had ever felt that before.

Many people love me and have loved me through many stages of my life, but I had never put myself in a situation where I had taken so much off the trophy case that I was left empty-handed with nothing to show. It was liberating and life-changing.

That kind of love changes a person from the inside out.

That kind of love shows us that there is a way to find connection and contentment.

Las Mujeres Increibles taught me about presence, support, and loving tenderly. They taught me that bigger is not necessarily better and that quiet is okay. They showed me how to be a good friend and how to receive. And they did it all by being themselves. We were a group of incredible women *being incredible by being ourselves.*

I returned to the U.S. with a confident quietude. Achievement for achievement's sake—was not it. Connection and contentment were it.

Incredible.

I am a museum full of art
but you had your eyes shut.
—Rupi Kaur

DESPERTI

We pack our backpacks. We are ready to hike! Anthony is at the front door of our Panamanian rental; he's ready before I am. I take more time than I need to make sure my hair is curled. The girls are crying what seem like real tears, and it's all I can do not to go back inside and make them waffles. Walking out the front door feels like a feat all its own. I know I'll miss my two daughters, but I also miss my husband and myself. I hop in the car, take deep breaths, and reach for Anthony's hand. We're headed to the mountains near Playa Coronado.

Being a mom means needing eight arms but only having six. Being a mom is wrestling with guilt every time you leave the house without your kids. But being a woman and a wife is feeling guilt and reminding yourself that there are other essential needs, too.

The roads to the mountains are slick. The trees are lush and damp, and the clouds are beginning to clear. We're on our way to *La India Dormida*, a mountain in Panama that resembles a silhouette of an indigenous woman sleeping. She is verdant with vibrant trees and tropical blossoms. The very look of her is welcoming. She is sleeping, but she is alive.

We stop by the local market, browse colorful trinkets, and start to ask for directions to the foot of the mountain. My neck is craned toward some colorful earrings when I see a man approaching me out of the corner of my eye. I'm a woman in a foreign country, so I tense up. But I remember I'm a woman with her husband, and I relax again. The tension comes from years of feeling unsafe with men in public spaces.

He has good intentions and asks us if we'd like a hiking guide. He knows we're not locals, so he inflates the price—an entire day with a hiking guide for $25, $10 more than the local discount.

We accept and follow him to the foot of the mountain, my heart rate increasing with every step. Our guide is wearing worn-in boat shoes. I'm a walking REI ad. Maybe I overdid it.

As we approach La India Dormida, I look around

in awe of God's majesty—the pure awesomeness and beauty of this slice of the world. I'm surrounded by a thousand shades of green—a rainbow of greens and more trees than I can count. The sun is barely peeking through in some corners of the Central American nation; in others, it's lighting up swaths of the jungle. Everything is alive, with toucans talking to each other, birds singing, and crickets chirping from tree to tree.

We make our way up La India's edges, our hearts beating, reminding us that we aren't in as good of shape as we thought. We feel droplets of rain that have miraculously made it through the multiple canopies, landing on our heads. Just enough to cool us off. We negotiate slick terra-cotta-colored mud, small rocks, and boulders carpeted with dense green clumps of moss. Even the moss is a marvel unto its own, illuminated with gradients of green in each tiny growth. I take on the energy of the phenomena around me. I begin to beam.

It's so easy to forget that this exists. It is so easy to get buried in the dishes, running to the store for toilet paper and emails, that we forget the magic right outside our front door.

Just at arm's length, Earth is waiting for us to interact with her—to stand in admiration of her complexity and her natural beauty. As I walk, I remember that she isn't only here to serve us in the form of resources; she is also here to be beautiful, to make our hearts feel good, to be admired, and to be cared for, much like we are.

As I walk, La India breathes into me, rejuvenating my spirit in a way that nothing else has ever been able to do. I'm walking her curves, feeling her form, and taking in the coolness of her clean waters: I am with God. It feels like God is all around me and inside my spirit simultaneously. I can't tell whether it's La India or whether it's God. Maybe it's a confluence, and maybe it's okay that it's a mystery. I feel magical.

And then I hear it before I see it—a rushing waterfall pouring into a small lagoon. I want to stand under it, but I shut myself down thinking of logistics. Wet leggings. Soggy underwear. I didn't bring a towel. But my spirit is dissatisfied. The thought reappears like a cat determined to reach a treat from the top of a cabinet. Anthony cheers me on, "Go for it, my love. You've got this!" He has so much faith in me. I see his optimism and decide to meet it.

I ask our hiking guide to stop.
I spot a boulder big enough to use as a table and a bench.

I take off my tennis shoes and sweaty socks.
I immediately feel the cool embrace of La India.

I step toward her waterfall, her roar drowning my thoughts with each inch forward. My toes curling to grip the contours of the rocks beneath me.
I get closer, feeling the power of her rushing water.

I press my chest against the sheets of water, meeting her, feeling her against my body. I'm going for it. I duck my head in, feeling the water drop 40 feet from the cliff's edge and explode onto my scalp. The water is cold. Powerful. It claps against my head, my neck, my back, my skin. Every sense is heightened. I am exhilarated, alive, and admiring her majesty.

The crashing water starts to get painful, so I trek back to my wadded-up socks and shoes and catch my breath.

I am in deep reverence for La India, for Mother Earth. I do not speak.
I am in awe.
There is nothing to say when there aren't proper words.

I am full.
I have been washed clean, inside the glory of God.

My spirit has awoken in the curves of La India Dormida.

I am far away from everything and right where I need to be. From afar, she looks gentle and welcoming and even simple. But as I got to know this majestic mountain, I learned there was so much more—so much power and nuance. Her beauty and presence ignited power and nuance within me.

Life is like this. We wake. We walk. We sleep. And sometimes we sleep while we wake and walk, numbing ourselves to the world around us, to the interconnectedness of it all and to our calling to participate in creation.

When we appreciate the greatness of Mother Earth and listen to the voice inside our hearts, we remember who we are—a *gentle return*.

May you listen.
May you step under the waterfall in your path.
May you be willing to wake up to your life.

Train in the art of satisfaction.
—Cheryl Strayed

CHOOSING SLOW
SUMMER 2018

As parents of young children, everyone advised us to *savor the moment* and enjoy the girls. We heard things like, "childhood will go by in a flash" and "don't miss it." My husband, Anthony, and I looked at each other and thought, *we'd better listen.*

We made a plan to slow down. We would take things off our plates. We would choose to be with our two young girls and cherish the days. We chose to leave our beloved Austin, Texas, and put our careers on hold to take a sabbatical from the grind of life. We'd choose to relocate our family somewhere where life was slow and we could be together.

Anthony and I gave away half of our belongings, stored the rest, and moved to Panama. My husband did all the planning, and I packed our bags. I didn't do a lick of research. I just trusted. We felt a sense of urgency to slow down, so the transition to Central America moved quickly.

Our family landed on Panamanian soil sight unseen. Our family of four arrived with six suitcases, two car seats, a stroller, a three-and-a-half-year-old and a one-and-a-half-year-old.

Anthony assured me he had arranged for a *luxury van* to take us to a hotel. I saw no luxury vans when we walked out of the airport and into the overwhelming humidity. I did see some janky vans. "That one!" Anthony was pointing to the janky van. *Oh my God,* I thought. The van did not accommodate our car seats. *Great. I'm in a foreign country and can't keep my babies safe. What did we get ourselves into?* My mind ping-ponged back to all of the First World comforts we left behind and gave away.

When we arrived in Coronado, a beach community about an hour outside Panama City, I felt this urge to be productive and busy because that's how I had always operated. But there was nothing to do in Coronado, a sleepy beach town. We had the beach, a gym, and golf. I had three choices.

And so I taught myself to sit and relax and not rush

from place to place. After all, there were only three options. It took our family about three months to settle in.

Eventually, we each learned a new way of life.
A slow way of life. And then, magic started to happen.

Anthony and I became more attuned to our daughters. We spent days truly seeing our girls for who they really were. We learned better ways to parent. We began to accomplish what we endeavored to do—we enjoyed our girls.

Countless hours were spent in the pool as we sought relief from the heat. The coolness of the wind swept over us as we swung in the handmade hammock crafted by local artisans. And we danced in the kitchen surrounded by fresh fruit plucked from neighborhood trees. Anthony and I chose to change the dynamic of our family. We learned how to be intentional with our words and our time, and we witnessed our girls flourish because of it.

Once the four of us found our bearings, we settled in and built a community.

Coronado became our home. We became friendly with Manuel, a fruit stand operator, the beach club staff, and the local hairdresser, Aldo. I accepted a part-time job as a fitness instructor and even became certified to teach Zumba. Anthony surfed and learned jiu-jitsu. We hosted barbeques, game nights, and play dates. We set out to love and connect with new people, and our friends and community loved us back.

WINTER 2018

We watch our girls light up, laugh during tickle fights, and pretend that bedtime is actually a suggestion. It's some of the most fun we have as a family. We moved to Panama and thought we'd stay for six months or maybe a year. But the time along Panama's southern coast was so sweet and precious. We just kept extending our stay. *Just a little while longer. Just a little while longer. We aren't ready for this season to end.*

Because of our choices, we get to savor slow mornings and slow afternoons with our girls. We don't have to share them with the world if we don't want to. A weekly swim class and jiu-jitsu are always optional in my mind. There's nowhere we need to be except here with each other.

We can do everything.
We can do nothing.
We get to decide.

It's March 2019, and we still have a year left. *Maybe a little more, a little more.* I am already lamenting the loss of our ability to spend time with our precious daughters—cuddle them and hug them when I want.

When we return to the U.S., my daughters will be older and will have school and commitments. There will be traffic and trips to the store and the gym, and our days will get parceled out. *Why do we have to live like that?*

Maybe we won't have to? Maybe we don't have to go back to our old way of living? Maybe we can rewrite the script of what it means to be a young family in America.

I have a hunch that we have evolved beyond our old way of busyness and hurry. But I'm unsure how to stay still with the world swirling around me. *I'll try my best to be with my girls; to be a witness to their lives; to the becoming and unfolding of their souls; to abide with them and give them the best I have to offer.*

I won't always get it right, but I absolutely cherish my daughters, Alexandra and Luciana, and I will always cherish *us*. I value the opportunity to love, guide, enjoy, steward, and cheer on my family. It brings me great joy and fulfillment to lead them to joy, watch them experience life in its fullness, mend their hearts, and remind them of how lucky the world is to have them.

Our stint in Panama will eventually come to an end, but maybe the *spirit* of the trip does not have to end. *Could that be possible?* Maybe I will be so familiar with what our version of *good* feels like that I will know impostors when they knock on my door. Maybe I'll be able to stay connected and keep it slow and simple. *Wouldn't that be nice?*

AUTUMN 2019

Alexandra is five, and Luciana is rounding the corner on three. It's time to pack our bags and return to Texas.

We have had a rough several months here. Anthony and Luciana's health has taken a turn. And a few nights ago, our home was broken into *while we were sleeping*. Even still, I am still so glad we came.

We did it.
We did it.

I mean, I'm a woman from a small town on the south Texas border. I grew up in the same three-bedroom house my entire childhood. Packing up and moving to a developing country is a big deal for me.

And I did it.
I figured it out.

I figured out traffic and directions. I figured out how to teach a fitness class in Spanish! I figured out healthcare and the school system. I learned how to build a community, one intentional act at a time.

Today, I told some friends we would be returning to the U.S., and one of my girlfriends said, "What are we going to do without your light?" She squeezed me tight. I cried.

Never in my wildest dreams did I picture our life sabbatical would unfold like this. We did exactly what we intended. We slowed down and loved Alexandra and Luciana well. It was an experience rich in love and courage. Our family is all the better for this *gentle return*. What an adventure.

I know someone is out there right now, wondering if they should take their own leap. They are wondering because their soul knows it needs to stretch. Their soul knows that when we leap, there is so much to be experienced, learned, felt, and enjoyed.

I don't know how their leap will turn out. It may not be a fairy tale, but after landing on solid ground after my own leap of faith, I know they will be delighted when they realize their strength and capability.

I hope they go for it.
I hope they come back and tell me the story.

The nature of this flower is to bloom.
—Alice Walker

MAMA, WHAT IS BEAUTY?

Growing up, I thought there were *beautiful* and *not-so-beautiful* people, and it was clear to me that beautiful people were valued more. I remember when I was ten-years-old, looking in the mirror and thinking I was short and chubby, wishing I was different. By the time I was in high school, culture's idea of beauty had solidified inside of me, tall, light skin, light hair, slender, round colored eyes—and since I didn't possess those qualities, I fell into thinking that I wasn't beautiful and not as valuable.

When I became a mother, I was still insecure about my body image. My oldest daughter, Alexandra, and motherhood were the catalysts for me to begin to come into my own and find my confidence. I wanted Alexandra to grow up feeling self-assured, confident, and beautiful, so I began my journey of self-discovery and healing.

I was so afraid of placing too much importance on my daughter's looks—even as a baby—that I placed none. I made sure that no one commented on her appearance—good or bad. People would say how beautiful she was or how amazing her golden-brown ringlets were, and I would shut them down. I'd instead navigate them toward words like healthy, strong, and smart. This went on for years.

When Alexandra was three, I was busy folding warm, fresh-from-the-dryer laundry. She was keeping me company and watching cartoons and one of the colorful characters squeaked out, "There's so much beauty!" This caught her attention, and she looked over at me and asked, "Mama, what is beauty?"

In a split second, I felt the weight of the moment. *Wow. I get to do this. I get to help mold her thoughts and her mind. This is my opportunity to pave an empowered way for her.* I called on God. *God, help me get to the crux of my sentiment with grace, clarity, and kindness. Amen.*

I put down the tiny toddler socks, looked at her, and answered, "Beauty is something that makes our hearts feel good. If it makes your heart feel good, it is beautiful."

It felt like I had dodged a bullet. But why? Had she never heard the word beauty? And then it sank in. I had let the pendulum swing the other way. In a warped way, I projected my own fears and insecurities onto my daughter, even though that's the very thing I was trying to avoid.

I had been parenting from a wound.

When I realized this, my heart sank. I realized that I didn't have to focus on outer beauty but could also acknowledge it and fold it in. I didn't have to be so afraid of noticing and appreciating it. For so long, I had a crushingly narrow definition of beauty. My definition was directly tied to who I saw on red carpets. As a child of the 80s and 90s, my gold standard of beauty were Cindy Crawford and Julia Roberts—everyone else was playing for silver. Some of my juvenile definition had to do with the simpleness of a child's mind, some with culture, and some with personal experience. *Who did all the girls at school think was pretty? Who did everyone know was beautiful? What were their lives like compared to the rest of us?*

Alexandra's very first definition of beauty is a definition that took me 32 years to even entertain. Thirty-two years for me to allow the possibility that beauty, as it relates to people, may have something to do with aesthetics—but it primarily has to do with the underlying spirit of a person, their heart, their energy. Thirty-two years for me to articulate what beauty truly means to *me*. Instead of letting beauty be defined by opinions and external characteristics, I began to let feelings, internal sensations, and experiences define beauty.

For me, beauty is being with my friend Nicky and laughing at the absurdity of our children rolling around on the floor.

Beauty is feeling the bigness of myself when I stand in front of a crowd.

Beauty is my cheeks spreading from side to side, revealing all my teeth when I'm genuinely joyful.

Beauty is feeling the shining sun, the wind sweeping against my skin, and my fingers clacking a keyboard.

Beauty is a pink dress, big earrings, and winking at my husband from across the room.

Beauty is something that makes my heart feel good.

My definition of beauty continues to get more inclusive.

As I write this, I feel good about who I am. I feel good about my beauty on the inside and out. I don't have to be afraid of it, nor do I have to chase it.

Emily Dickinson reminds us that, "Beauty is not caused. It is."

Because of this, I can give my daughters a broader perspective of beauty than I absorbed as a child. I am conscious of not projecting my fears onto them. I am giving my daughters what I consider to be a powerful gift: an expansive and even open-ended definition of beauty that they can own, not one they have to reach for.

I can look in the mirror now and feel proud to stand in my body, my spirit, and in my beauty. And I am proud to see my daughters standing proudly, right next to me.

Believing is a big part of doing.
—Unknown

MY HAIR, MY BODY

One of my first paid jobs was as a bartender. I would make drinks, create good conversation, and flirt—for a bigger tip. Maybe I could squeeze an extra $20 out of a customer or even the elusive $100. I played the game. I used myself, my energy, my hair, my body, and my attention to get tips.

I don't have shame about it, but I do have great sadness for the girl who thought that was the way to have value, to be seen, and to have power. In that environment, I started to base my worth on how much a man would spend on me. The more money a man spent, the more pride I felt.

If a guy looked at me, ogled me, cracked slightly lewd jokes—it's grimy, but I would think—*I'm in. I've got 'em*. And then it was only a matter of time until we figured out what the relationship would look like. It was survival of the fittest, and I was surviving.

I remember going on dates and afterward feeling like I owed men sex—I owed them my body because they had bought me a meal or taken me out for a show.

As a woman, I was raised to give, serve, and be hospitable—to cushion the blow for everyone else. To absorb feelings of discomfort so that others could be more comfortable. I could have said, "thank you for the evening," and gone home, but giving my body was always easier than sharing my truth.

It was a low bar, and they were sad transactions. I would feel detached from my body, my heart, and my feelings. I barely felt like I owned what I was giving away.

On the outside, I looked fine and acted fine, but on the inside, I was always scared. If life were a sport, I was playing injured. I walked around with fresh wounds that I would cover and overlook.

I want my daughters to have a different experience regarding their bodies. I want them to have complete autonomy and be comfortable standing in their power. Anthony and I teach them to honor their bodies in many ways—to have dominion over their bodies—to treat them with care and respect.

When Alexandra was in kindergarten, I went to sweep her hair in a ponytail while she was dressing for school. She said, "My hair, my body! You don't have permission."

It stopped me in my tracks. Here I was, her mother, helping her get ready to go out and experience the day. I knew that if I overrode her voice, eventually, she would find it harder to keep centered and firm in her conviction. I knew that, at the moment, I was teaching and reinforcing a lesson about body autonomy. About how her body—including her hair and everything else about her—is her domain. It is, in the end, hers.

Some people may think, *you're her mom and you were getting her ready for school. You can override her. She was being so sassy!*

I took a second to breathe. "You're right," I said, "I did not have permission." I stepped back and asked, "Alexandra, would it be okay if I gave you a ponytail?"

"Yes." And we proceeded.

I will always have some sense of authority over Alexandra and Luciana—after all, I am their mother—but I believe it is my job to help them claim and choose for themselves. A lot of other people throughout my daughter's lives will also have opinions, claims, and desires about what my daughters should do with their bodies. And I want them to know that no one's opinion or preference matters more than their own.

This is the power of learning and internalizing bodily autonomy for us women. What another person wants does not matter more than what you want. You may not always be able to get what you want, but what you want should always matter. All good relationships are built on love, respect, and trust, where both people are significantly valued.

The mother/daughter relationship is the perfect chance to explore what a good relationship looks like and feels like.

What does a loving, caring, solid relationship look like? What does it feel like? How do two people dance it out? How does someone lead with honor? What does it feel like when two people want the best for themselves and one another?

"This is my hair and my body." Yes, it is, my sweetheart. Yes, it is.

Women find their way back to themselves not by
moving up and out into the light like men,
but by moving down into the depths
of the ground of their being.
—Maureen Murdock

YOU ARE MY BUCKET LIST

I have always felt called to live a great life, though a "great life" has meant different things at different times.

As a young girl flipping through a magazine, one advertisement caught my eye. A svelte ballerina—her hair tied back in a bun, head bowed in contemplation—cloaked in the darkness of a navy velvet theater curtain. The ad read, "Greatness comes with a price." I cut it out without consulting anyone and made it my North Star. I would be great, and I knew it would cost me. Before I knew what one was, *this* was my bucket list.

As a high school senior, I journaled and wrote,

I seriously need to make friends. I don't know; it's weird. My classes are alright, nothing I can't handle;

that Salutatorian spot will be mine; it will be. I have to make a speech, and I'm going to give it my all; I'll even take Adderall. Thank you, God, for today and for my family's health and happiness.

When I arrived at The University of Texas at Austin as a freshman, I arrived with the thought that I was going to follow a pre-medical course track. The fact that I hated math and science didn't matter. Pre-med was the fanciest, most applause-worthy thing a freshman could say—so that's what I said. I knew enough to know that I needed to play the game well, and that was the next right move. Then, I figured out I would have thousands of hours of math and science ahead of me, so I pivoted. I didn't know what I wanted to be, so I picked the next fanciest, most applause-worthy college program before pre-law. Bless my 18-year-old heart. School started, and since I had enrolled in UT's business school—all my friends were studying business, and they seemed fine—I eventually chose marketing.

And that's how I made a lot of my life decisions. What's the fanciest, most applause-worthy thing? I'd then point my toes in that direction.

It has always been an easy enough formula. Sometimes I achieve or I get it, and sometimes I don't. When I reach it, I feel like, *Okay, good—we're on track! We are doing this thing called LIFE.* And when I don't achieve it, I think, *I'm not working hard enough. I need to try harder. Maybe I don't have what it takes?* It's like my congratulatory self has never met my motivated-by-meanness self.

When I became a mother, I felt like I was being pulled in two directions: career and home. And not just any career—a grand career. One where I would wield a microphone and energy in an arena and speak to thousands at a time. And for the longest time, the forces pulling me in each direction felt like they were tearing me apart. There was no place for peace in between. No bucket could hold both at once.

When we lived in Panama, I began to unravel all of this and became aware of my motivations. One day, I was reading about one of my role models, and I watched her wield a microphone and speak to thousands of women at a time, and I thought,

I don't want to pay the price she is paying. I don't want to get on airplanes all the time. I don't want to be away from my kids like that. I don't want to strive in that way.

It was the first time I had ever thought anything but *BE THE BEST*, and that was weird. *Was this how I felt? Or was I just lazy and complacent?*

We moved back to Texas from Panama, and soon after, the COVID-19 pandemic turned the world upside down. I became acutely aware of how fragile life is. Death and tragedy were all around, and there was no rhyme or reason—no way to explain or justify it. Things were bad for some people and not as bad for others. Not because some people were bad, but because hurt and heartache knocks on all our doors. No one is exempt.

I started to think, *if I'm only here for a certain amount of time, if Anthony is only here for a certain amount of time, if my kids can be taken from me for no reason, I'd better make the most of the time I have with them.*

This sounds morbid, but it's the truth.
None of us are guaranteed a damn thing.
In the blink of an eye, our lives can change.

My husband's chronic illness has often pushed our family to the brink. This part of our lives has significantly shaped us and has made me stronger as a woman and mother and more able than I ever thought I would have to be.

I had a business coach/astrology session a few months into the pandemic. On the call, my coach asked me to envision myself speaking to thousands of people from a stage. She asked me to imagine what I was wearing, how I felt, and what it sounded like. And then she asked me, "How do you feel right now?" I said, "I have a knot in my stomach."

"Is it because you're scared of that moment?" "No," I replied. "But if I'm on stage, my kids are home without me."

On the one hand, I thought I was supposed to go after the fanciest and most applause-worthy thing, and on the other hand, I didn't want to pay the price for eventually achieving that thing. These were the two directions: Be a mom in the way I want or have a big, fancy career.

This is not to say that my experience is what everyone should or does feel; it's only to say that I feel. A few months later, I was at a Christmas party making new friends. After a bit of conversation, someone said, "You're the most interesting person I've met this year." My heart swelled. "Thank you." And I started to think about my life.

I am studying marriage and family therapy. I work with people I love through my business, Bright Light. I make a difference in people's hearts and their families and homes. I love my husband. I have two kids that I love and enjoy. I have a space heater for my feet underneath my desk and dark chocolate after the kids go to sleep. I have breath in my lungs—and sometimes, I even have a fun polish color on my fingernails. I spend most of my time doing what I want, which is a huge blessing. But then, I consider the other direction, no microphone, no arena.

Is it a failure?
Complacency?
Or a choice?

A few weeks after the Christmas party, my family got sick from what we thought was COVID, and I was reminded of how fragile life is. Again. It was Anthony's third time with the virus, Alexandra's second, and Luciana's first. My heart was breaking, and I prayed and pleaded for guidance. And as God does, God sent me guidance through Kate Bowler.

Kate Bowler is a Professor of Divinity at Duke University, an author and a podcaster. She writes from the perspective of a woman, wife, and mom diagnosed with stage 4 cancer. She has dealt with heartbreak, tragedy, and grief, and she shares it in a way that few do. During a podcast, she shared that she had made a sign for her husband and son: YOU ARE MY BUCKET LIST. She wanted them to know that she loves them and wants to be WITH them.

So many times, we hear about bucket lists for traveling, building businesses, and physical challenges—we don't often hear about bucket lists for relationships. Kate said it was okay to center your life on people and relationships. *What? Was that allowed?* That's not fancy or applause-worthy. There's no arena or microphone. Centering your life on people and relationships is everyday life.

At that moment, the chasm that I felt for my entire motherhood vanished. It's like someone was permitting me to love my home life and be satisfied with my husband, kids, and family.

Yes, I thought. *This feels right.*

I cried tears of relief. My shoulders dropped. I settled into the notion that my life was good, and it was okay for me not to want anything else—not feel like there was a void.

I went home and shared it with Anthony. I told him about Kate Bowler and the notion, YOU ARE MY BUCKET LIST. I told him that our life and our home *were my bucket list* and that I wanted to be with him.

My head was laying on a pillow, tears running sideways, and I was telling him how I always thought that "people"—*God knows who these people are because I couldn't name ONE . . . but PEOPLE*—were going to think I chose motherhood as a cop-out. I told him I thought *people* would think I couldn't make it as a fancy applause-worthy person, so instead, I focused on being a mom. I don't remember how he replied because it was such a relief to get those feelings out of my body where they had been rotting and festering. I let it all go.

I want my time with my family to be intentional— to matter. I don't want to look back on my life and realize that I missed it because I was lamenting about some imaginary thing I thought I needed to do. What a shame it would be to miss all the blessings in front of me for a belief or expectation that I absorbed along the way. Instead, I can choose to be present with, satisfied with, and even proud of my choice.

I can set down the image of the ballerina in the darkness—in solitude—paying her price. I can create my own image—my own bucket that I can fill how I choose, with what I choose. *But what does it mean to choose a new way of being in the world? What is the price of believing in a new way? What's the price of redefining greatness or letting that word go altogether?*

Beliefs are powerful. They can lift us or tear us down. They can make us feel good or make us feel crazy. It is scary to let go of a belief because it feels like a free fall. It feels like,

I've done it this way for so long that I can't afford to let it go. What if my belief is true, and I fall flat on my face, and people reject me? What if I let go of the belief and suffer the pain of not belonging?

I know these thoughts and how scary they can be. For me, the scariest lies my ego tells me are: *What if I am ordinary? What if I am not special?* Those lies go to the core for me. And so, letting those lies go was like letting go of a life vest, believing that my ego is wrong and trusting that my true self can swim.

Further, it's like a way of saying, *I am enough. My life is enough. What I give is enough. I am not worthy because of what I do; I am worthy because I am.*

My friend, are you doing something FOR worth, or are you doing it FROM worth? FOR or FROM? In my work with my clients, I often teach from this vantage point. This is a staple of my teaching. I teach it because I have worked through all sorts of layers within myself, figuring out why I do what I do and letting my unaligned parts slough off.

Sometimes, these realizations take time and experience. I'm not sure I would have gotten here without many heartaches. There's something so transformative about heartache—it makes you raw, vulnerable, and connected. It pushes you to figure out what matters to you and why, and reminds you that life is precious. Could I have known this at 18 or 25? I don't think so, and that's okay—different lessons were learned then.

You're not alone if you feel like you are being pulled in different directions. If you feel like *fancy and applause-worthy things* are the path for you, go for it—you're not alone. If you feel like a quiet, patched-together life in yoga pants and reading sentimental books to your kids is the path for you, go for it—you're not alone.

There is no one at the finish line handing out worthiness certificates. Nothing we do can MAKE us worthy. No degree, business, relationship, body weight, or career can shift any of us into worthiness. No imaginary crowd is waiting on the other side of the curtain to applaud us. There is only a mirror where we will see ourselves reflected through our own eyes—real and raw. The worthiness comes from the inside—it's the starting point. And good news: you're there. You're worthy because—*you are*. Women are worthy because—*we are*. Realizing that you are already worthy *is a gentle return*.

I have always felt like I was meant for great things.
And now I have them.
Because I choose them.

I am the one making my own bucket list.
And, I know exactly who and what is on it.

The soul becomes dyed with
the color of its thoughts.
—Marcus Aurelius

———————————

HANDS ON CHEEKS

"With every breath, you're getting more relaxed; with every breath, you're getting more and more comfortable. The more you listen to my voice, the more you'll go into a deep sense of calm."

It's my fourth hypnosis session, and I'm familiar with the unfamiliar. These sessions are disarming because there is no road map, no guarantee. It's an agreement to dive into my subconscious and explore like a deep-sea diver sinking through ocean water in inky darkness. Each time, there is a level of fear because, of course, there are creatures in the ocean that could take you down, or maybe it's just a seashell. My level of trust beats out my fear by only the slightest margin. I am in this insane predicament–diving into my subconscious—terrified and tired.

Today, I love my life. I am married to a man I love

deeply. I have two children that I adore. I am safe and comfortable. And yet, my thoughts wander back to the chaos I experienced while engaged to someone else more than a decade ago. I don't want these old thoughts mingling in my brain with things like volunteering at my daughters' school and planning family vacations. These old thoughts keep parts of me oriented to the past, and I am sick of carrying the extra weight. Every thought about that season in my mid-twenties feels like an intruder jumping out from behind a door—BOO!

What is wrong with me? If that relationship is long over, why are the wounds still present? I am embarrassed and ashamed that more than 10 years later, I cannot get over it. So, I've turned the dial from talk therapy to hypnosis—anything for relief.

"I want you to think of a beautiful space—somewhere you feel safe and comfortable."

Here we go. I picture an open field where a forest of oak trees lies on the horizon. Like hazy layers, I see frosty blues, deep greens, and grass, the color of sand.

"Now, I invite you to place a bench in the beautiful space. And I want you to picture your younger self right after you learned to play the game."

Diving deeper, seeing less.

I was attuned to what people wanted and expected from me from an early age. As a daughter of a Mexican-born mother and a Mexican father, things like hard work, sacrifice, and excellence were a given. These values were so ingrained that they were never spoken of—they were embodied. Flowers bloom. Birds fly. Mexicans work hard.

Like all young hearts, mine thirsted for praise, validation, and acceptance, so I did what I thought I needed to do to receive it. I set goals that I thought other people wanted for me, and I knocked them down one by one. I achieved in school, extracurriculars, looks, language, and manners—it was my autopilot. I was playing a game, exchanging achievement for worth, but I didn't know it.

My mind flashes to when I was eight and in the third grade. My chestnut hair was short with the ends curled under; my cheeks were flush and full. I wore a popsicle-orange and purple colored jumper, my favorite outfit then. My eyes were filled with an undercurrent of fear and confusion, veiled with eagerness as I tried so hard to connect with my classmates. My eight-year-old thoughts were racing. *Am I doing this right? This is so hard. I want to belong.*

I feel like an outsider. What's happening to my body? Why does being eight feel like it comes easier to other people? Why do I feel so awkward? I'll keep working harder. My little face and heart contained so many unanswered questions.

My middle-aged heart shatters open for that little eight-year-old. *Why did she think she had to have things figured out? How could she possibly know the answers to any of those questions? Those were not for her to answer—or her responsibility. She was eight. Eight.*

"And now I'd like you to invite your wise self to the bench. The part of you that you can trust. Maybe your wise self looks like an angel or an elderly woman, or maybe she doesn't look any way in particular—maybe it's more of a feeling."

I conjure a wise self who is an ethereal creature: golden wings, graceful curves, a gentle glow, a warmth to her presence.

"Would it be okay if eight-year-old Catia and your wise-self hold hands?"

I nod, reaching around for tissues, trying not to open my eyes and disrupt the moment.

"Now, wise self, turn to eight-year-old Catia and cup her tender cheeks in your hands. See all her confusion, tumult, anxiousness, anticipation, eagerness, and wanting. Send her love and adoration for who she is. Let her know she doesn't have to work so hard or achieve to impress anyone anymore—she can rest. She wants so badly to impress people and be seen and validated—but that's all over now—that's not for her to do anymore. Your wise self is going to love eight-year-old Catia well."

By age 22, I had earned undergraduate and graduate degrees and managed a restaurant full-time. Getting into a serious relationship and getting married seemed like the next logical step. I was young, in love, and hopeful. Since everything looked good, I bypassed the fact that a part of me didn't feel good. That decision to ignore my inconvenient feelings turned my life upside down.

Right then, the hypnotist helps me put a lifetime of wanting to achieve and wanting to perform well into perspective. *Oh, checking the proverbial next box was a coping mechanism. I just wanted to be loved.*

Children need love and attention and will adjust however they need to connect.

"Feel her tender cheeks, gaze into her almond-shaped

brown eyes, and send your eight-year-old Catia uncondi-tional love and adoration. She's loved just the way she is."

I am barely able to catch my breath between sobs. *Wait, I can rest? I have nothing to prove? I am already loved?*

The session wraps. I am shaken and skeptical. I look around my life, playing with these new notions but not yet accepting them. Accepting them means slowing down. It means being unguarded. It means I could get hurt. *What if the hypnotist is wrong? What if I'm not already loved? What if I do have to earn it?* I've been hurt enough, and I decide the risk is worth it. I can always return to earning; I already know how to operate that way.

I am not committing; I am experimenting. I begin to make small decisions from a place of knowing I am worthy and loved. *What do I want to eat? What clothes do I want to wear? Who do I want to call back?* I am diving into the dark, and it is disorienting.

Am I doing this *from* worth, or am I doing it *for* worth?

If the answer is *for* worth, I gently thank my eight-year-old self for working so hard and remind myself that I am already loved and can rest. At first, it feels like hooey. *This is crap. This blurs all the lines and takes away so much that I'm used to it.*

The certainty that I'm loved actually creates more uncertainty in my life.

But I keep going.

Slowly, I begin to align. I'm easier going around the house, paying less attention to organizing the perfect party favors, and taking on fewer responsibilities. *Can I fulfill that volunteer position? Yes. Do I want to add that to my spinning plates? No.*

With intention, I stop laboring over my life *looking* a certain way and pay more attention to my life *feeling* a certain way.

Going into hypnosis helped break the decades-long spell of ingrained beliefs about my self-worth. When I let my awareness sink into the inky depths, there were indeed creatures, but they were parts of me— not there to hurt me but needing love. I needed to learn to love and accept myself. Once I realized how deep that ocean goes and what it feels like for my wise self to hold the cheeks of my terrified eight-year-old self, I was free.

I was the ocean, and I was the creatures and the freedom.

I was whole.

Now, in my day-to-day life, I carry myself differently. At first, the fact that there was no road map to a hypnosis session scared me—I had always followed the maps I'd inherited. Now, I am learning daily that when there is no map, I am not lost: I am sovereign.

I have the agency to listen to myself and choose where I want to go.

Sometimes, when I look at my daughters, I am overwhelmed by how much I love them. I place my hands on their cheeks and tell them I love, adore and delight in them, just as they are—and I mean it.

I want to give my daughters a knowing of their *enoughness*. I want those beliefs to inhabit their oceans.

And sometimes, in the warm glow of the morning light, I look at my own face in the mirror, and cup my own cheeks. I close my eyes and listen to the golden voice of my wise self, who reminds me to love every part of me.

As I embrace myself, I am whole and free again.

Confident people—do.
—Luciana Elizabeth Holm

COLD PLUNGE

Halloween 2022 was approaching, and there was a chill in the Central Texas air. I was on the back porch of our home, hunched over, badmouthing my daughters in the privacy of my head, as I picked up random hair ties and swimsuits. My back had been aching for weeks. *Age*, I figured. Nothing was helping: not muscle relaxers, not yoga, not chiropractors. Nothing. I felt the creak in my knees as I felt the pool beckon.

If my saltwater pool had eyes, I would have avoided eye contact. Sometimes, we know something is calling us forward, but we're not ready, so we give it our backs. This was one of those times.

The next morning, as I walked out to proudly watch bright red cardinals eat from our newly filled bird feeder, I felt the pool call again. *Why is this pool messing with me?* I wondered.

After my morning tea, I popped two pain relievers and started assembling our family costumes. Distraction is always welcome when we are avoiding something.

Later, I looked out the kitchen window to the pool again, hoping it wouldn't catch me staring, and I smirked. *Damn.* I knew what I needed to do. I needed to get in. Not because it was warm but because it was cold.

I didn't know much about cold plunging, but I heard it was good for you. But they used to say that about diet soda, too. I knew that I liked a challenge, so I answered the call. I committed to one plunge.

I pulled out a faded bathing suit, popped in my earbuds, and found the loudest, most upbeat music available. The goal was for my 5'3 body to make it neck-deep into the pool for the length of one song.

I didn't want to do it.

But I knew I had to do it.

"Freedom is a state of mind; what ya gonna do with mine," pumped into my ears. *Right foot in. Left foot in.* The water started to ripple. *Knees in. Hips in. Ooooh, shoulders in.*

October's water temperature arrested me. I felt my chest compress. *Breathe . . . Breathe . . . In through the nose, out through the mouth*. My body was cold. My breath wanted to go faster and faster. *You can do anything for a few minutes, Catia . . . Just a little longer.* Then, the song ended.

As I stepped up and out from the pool, the fall wind transformed my olive-colored thighs scarlet red as goosebumps multiplied across my lower body. My teeth chattered. My hands shook. As I draped a towel over my shoulders, I thought, *I DID THAT*.

As my body vibrated, my spirit steadied. I felt terrific, instantly more powerful.

We can let ourselves feel good or get in our own way of that feeling.

As seasonal decorations transitioned from ghosts and goblins to turkeys and twinkle lights, I kept plunging. To my surprise, the music I chose transitioned over time, too. I started this experiment with intense, upbeat dance music to carry me through the cold and then eventually moved to gospel music before shifting to meditative melodies. Every time I dunked my body in cold water, I could feel my mental strength getting stronger. After a few weeks, the pain relievers returned to the cupboard.

By winter, I committed to doing a daily plunge, rain or shine. Freeze or not. Knowing that I would follow through every day was thrilling. The self-efficacy boost was intoxicating. It feels good to feel good.

My husband, Anthony, eventually joined me. Our curious daughters eventually took the plunge, too. One Saturday, Anthony and I were in the pool, intentionally breathing, when our eldest, Alexandra, chose to get in.

I watched her breathing stop and her eight-year-old chest contract—just like mine had the very first time I dipped my feet in. I walked through the cold water to reach her. I stared into her eyes.

"You've got this. Inhale, exhale. Inhale, exhale. You can get out whenever you want. You've got this."

Alexandra didn't scream or flail her arms. She invited the 40-degree salt water to rush over her body as she steadied her breathing with mine.

"That's it. You're strong. You're safe."

A mother and daughter, eyes locked and hearts connected. "Keep breathing, sweet girl. You're safe. I am with you."

"You're done," our youngest cheered as she timed our plunge from the warmth of the porch. "Five minutes, everyone!"

I hadn't ever thought about how Alexandra's first plunge would actually go, but I wasn't surprised by her choice to participate and commit. She and I have been connected her whole life. Mothers and daughters often ride the same waves, for better or worse.

As my first season of cold plunges extended, day after day, meditative music was traded for songs worth singing out loud.

Daytime plunges became nighttime plunges, and when the temperature dropped even lower—my power ballads morphed into concert performances. I could dance; I could punch and shimmy; and I could circle my hips—no one could see. The water moved with me. It was both liberating and protective. I could be who I wanted to be in water, and I could feel held.

I remembered my percussion roots, my childhood ballet recitals, and my natural Mexican rhythm. I felt strong, capable, and joyful in the water. With every plunge, I proved to myself that I was the kind of woman who prioritized feeling good.

When we learn to trust ourselves, the world becomes a safer place, even in near-freezing temperatures.

I started to crave the cold, its rush of dopamine, and the instant satisfaction of following through. My back pain was long gone. My anxiety decreased. My ability to focus increased. I began to feel light and bright in the winter haze.

Every once in a while, my daughters joined me. And every few nights, during a plunge, I'd gaze up at the moon, belt out a song, take up as much space as I wanted, and simultaneously feel my sensuality, strength, significance, and insignificance.

The daily ritual of cold plunging became a daily baptism—a touchstone, a remembering of who I am, how I want to feel, and who I want to be. It became a *gentle return*. A way to connect to who I am and a way to touch the life force that lives inside me.

This is what it means to reclaim my body, my heart, and myself. To make the *gentle return* to the heart of the woman I have always been—somehow both always changing and always the same.

Tentative but certain.
Exposed yet safe.
Frozen and free.

This is my feminine power.

At 39 years old, I am home, inside myself. Again.

There can be no happiness if the things we believe in are different from the things we do.
—Freya Stark

THE PROTOCOL

It's Wednesday. Family photos are on Saturday.

I've been preparing for a month. Everyone's outfits are coordinated and ready, except for mine. Why do women always make sure everyone is cared for before we begin caring for ourselves?

I am in my closet, reaching into the depths of the space to pull out dresses from another lifetime. I've been eating more veggies and passing on dessert the last few weeks, so I know these old dresses will slip right on. I also know that if I look good in our family photo, my perception of how I look daily will change.

One photo serves as confirmation: A*m I beautiful or not?*

My first choice is a dress fit for a princess. I step

into it, knowing it has a tricky closure that requires the strength of two to zip up. *I can do it. I will do it.* I hoist up my boobs with one arm, contort my other arm to reach my spine, and attempt to will the zipper up. Nothing. *I will not surrender.* I lay belly down on the carpet, the velvet navy blue princess dress pooling on the floor. Thrusting my body in all directions, like a sea lion, I attempt to squirm my way into the fabric. *Hold your breath.* Nope. *Deep breath. Up!* Nope. *Damn.*

Drowning in my navy sea, I wave the white flag.

I stand up. The dress drops to my ankles. I review my body. *You are 39. You have given birth to two children. Your ribs are wider. Your boobs are bigger. The last time you wore this dress, you were a fitness instructor. You are loved. You are healthy. Things change. Bodies change.* I am disappointed but not quite berating myself.

Good enough.

Our beauty standards haunt us like ghosts. We women are beautiful, healthy, and vibrant. We make the world a better place. We deliver new life to this world. And yet, we turn our attention to what we are not—to a constructed idea, decided by someone else, of how we fall short.

Thank goodness for Plan B. It fits.

I zip up. Twirl. Now, all four of us are prepared. I walk to the kitchen to refill my water and remember; *I have some allergy medication that suppresses my appetite!*

For 20 years, I have followed the same photo protocol. A few weeks before a photo shoot, I dial it in. I put a pause on wine and sweets and drink a lot of water. The week of the shoot, I take allergy medication, get my nails done, and ready my routine. A few days before, I exfoliate, do extra face masks, and prioritize sleep. On the day of the photo shoot, I am sparkling, just like I've been through the full-price car wash. It's all by design. I perversely objectify myself even though it erodes the very thing I want, to feel comfortable in my own skin. With every edit of myself, I subliminally send myself the message that I'm not good enough. I coerce myself into the notion that my value lies in my ability to squeeze myself into a fabricated standard of beauty.

But this time, it's different. I stare at the allergy medication and process a conveyor belt of questions: *Why do I want to take this? Where does this belief come from? Who says beauty and worthiness are only available at a dress size just out of reach?*

In this moment, I am trying to reconcile my beliefs about body image, my desire for how I want my daughters to feel, and what I teach clients. One little pill holds so much.

Instinctively, I put my hands on my heart and belly. I hold my body and say, *"I trust you. Whatever size you need to be is good. I know you have a reason for it."* I surrender the fight. I will not battle myself any longer.

When we love people right where they are, their shoulders and defenses drop, and they begin to expand. When someone loves us generously, it inspires us to love ourselves generously. Our posture shifts from wanting to achieve a sense of worthiness to a posture of someone who knows they are worthy. Someone who feels and knows they are worthy is loving, kind, creative, and bright.

They are not doing things for worth.
They do things from worth.

They know how special they are and that everything they do expresses their worth. They aren't striving for something or someone to deem them worthy. Instead, they are taking action and being who they want to be from a place of worth, knowing they are inherently divine and deserve goodness and grace.

At that moment, I decide enough is enough. I will love myself generously. I shut the kitchen drawer.

For a moment, I claim my power.
I make a decision from a place of worth instead of searching for it.

We will each have many different bodies during our lifetime: baby, toddler, young kiddo, teen, pregnant body, postpartum body, and then, maybe a mama body and hopefully an aging body. These phases are not better or worse than each other but constantly molten and transform. Each has its purpose, its meaning, and its own story.

To love our bodies is to honor each phase of our life. To love our bodies is to enjoy them for their health and gifts and then let go—because another version is coming.

As our bodies move from phase to phase, the world tries to focus its agendas on what we should wear and how we should experience our bodies. But our bodies are for honor, exploration, and tenderness. Everything else is a distraction. All our bodies are good, beautiful, and worthy of love, respect, and kindness.

The story of my body is my story.

The story of your body is your story.

I look at those family pictures now, and see myself standing beautiful, strong, and radiant with my family. I see my body as part of everything that I am. I see myself as I am, there at that moment, experiencing goodness. I see my *gentle return*.

When I choose to love myself and love my story, I am at home in my body. That is the photo protocol I want to trust even more.

Two roads diverged in a wood, and I—
I took the one less traveled by,
And that has made all the difference.
—Robert Frost

GUAPO LEAVING TOWN

Anthony's dusty Volvo is pulling out of the driveway. It's August 2022, and I am sobbing. Luciana is clinging to my leg. Alexandra's arms are wrapped around my hips. My daughters wipe their tears on my clothes. I am working double time, allowing myself to be sad but not so sad that it will scare the girls.

My husband, Anthony, who I have called Guapo since we started dating, had been seeking a career change and found it . . . a six-hour drive from our front door. He would be away from us Sunday to Friday for one year.

I've learned that a stable marriage requires nimbleness. Each member must make space for the other—to listen, allow, and encourage. This requires a constant reading of the partner, the marriage, and the family—even when it's hard, especially when it's hard.

Our family, by privilege and by choice, has, since its creation, been able to avoid typical 9 to 5 jobs. Anthony and I made it a priority to work, as much as possible, while our daughters were asleep or at school. Alexandra and Luciana have never known a world where they didn't see Mom or Dad while at home.

But today, their Papa is driving away. My heart is breaking the way a glass window shatters when hit by a rock. One big point of impact with hundreds of tiny cracks emanating from it. I've spent most of the last 10 years alongside this bearded, Midwestern man. And now, our family is trying something new. My heart is shattering, and it's excited. *Now, I'll get the remote control.*

As a Mexican-American woman, culture taught me that big worry equaled big love and that if I was happy while someone I loved was sad, my love wasn't true enough. During emotionally challenging times, it has always felt safer to lean into the expected emotion and bury the taboo, unseemly emotion. So, I communicate my sadness and bury my excitement.

Weeks into becoming a solo parent, I am physically and emotionally exhausted. I spend my time alerting teachers to our family's situation in anticipation of our children melting down. I am so new to solo parenting that I lead with, "my husband works out of town—so it's just me!" Trying to prepare people for the moment that I come undone. It's a strange shift. I am in charge of everything, all the time.

Days are hard. Juggling graduate school, my job, the kids' school, extracurriculars, and weekly trips to the pediatrician—is a lot. As I cram everything in, sleep shifts from necessary to optional. Soon, my body begins to break down.

But, as hard as the days are, the nights are lovely. I get to choose how to spend my time, even if it's soaking up reruns of *New Girl*. Without guilt, I keep all the lights off, turn them on, slather on face masks, or work out until 11 p.m. What I choose to do doesn't impact anyone. It has been at least 10 years since I knew that freedom and felt that spaciousness. It is both familiar and foreign. It feels like I'm cheating at a card game I'm playing alone.

As a woman growing up, I always lived in consideration of those around me. This can be a good thing, but if taken too far, it can be a detriment. I have always considered my parents, brothers, college roommates, and boyfriends before I considered myself. *What would they want me to do? Would they be uncomfortable if . . .? Was I inconveniencing them?* It made me the kind of person who colors inside the lines. In my late 20s, I had two glorious years of being single and living alone, so I vaguely remembered what it was like to make decisions solely on what I wanted. I just didn't remember how good it felt to make those decisions.

Life as a solo parent is challenging. There are runs to the E.R., plumbing emergencies, and logistical catastrophes. Somehow, I manage. The weekdays go by faster and faster. The situation is not becoming easier for our family, but it's becoming easier for me.

A few months in, the girls are asleep, and I am waiting to welcome Guapo home. I plop down on the couch—tired. I do the same routine every Friday night in the hours before he arrives. I empty the trash, wash dishes, and cook a warm meal. My level of fatigue feels extreme to me, so I follow it with curiosity. *Am I welcoming him or staging the house? Staging our lives?* His simple, Midwestern nature requires no artifice, *so why am I doing all of this? Why am I performing? Wait. Is that what I am doing—performing?*

Without announcement, I commit to experimenting with performing less. *Maybe it will be okay. Perhaps our family and our marriage will be okay without the show?*

Maybe I can be as comfortable with Anthony at home as I am with my daughters? It is an ease I am not sure is available in the presence of my husband. He's a man, after all, and my job as a woman is to serve him.

Bit by bit, I begin to see his new job and the 380 miles between us as a way to explore and reclaim the parts of me that I had pushed aside nearly a decade prior. One day, I admit to feeling guilty because I dropped the ball on cooking, and Luciana says, "We don't need some silly cooking; just be you." My mama heart swells at her spirit and wisdom. I begin liking the alone time and admitting to it. I reclaim going with the flow, cooking less, being loud, and blasting mariachi music.

The hardest part about feeling two opposing feelings is admitting it to ourselves and to others. We hold back and suppress because we fear being labeled bad people.

I have been so conditioned to serve that even though I know I can be myself—I don't need to live in reaction to Anthony or the shadow of his preferences—it's been hard to get there unless he's not there. I required physical space and time to practice. *Who was I absent of my husband? What did I value? What brought me joy? Was it possible to bring that self into my marriage?*

When we encounter challenges and experience life shifts, our insides change. Then we have to decide if we also want to change our outsides. Because sharing our insides on the outside can cause change we never see coming. Clarity on who we are and what we like can feel like asking waves to be still. Clarity, at times, feels almost impossible.

Being conscious that parts of who we are can be performative might be painful, complicated, and disorienting, but admitting who we truly are can give us a foundation that is much steadier. Being conscious of the parts that make us whole supports a life where joy is sustainable and real.

Winter holidays are upon us, and the comforting embrace of pine is in the air. I've had four months to settle into this new season. I take a big gulp and reach out for Guapo as he settles back into our home. "Honey, I've been noticing some things about myself . . ." I decide that our marriage can sustain this change, so I share my revelations, which he cheers on. "Yes, great! Be yourself! Don't worry about cooking. I am a grown man. I can feed myself."

My husband can feed himself, and so can I.

In exploring and embracing our individual needs and

desires, my husband and I can nourish ourselves and, in turn, our marriage. Sometimes, we cook for each other. Sometimes, no one cooks at all.

We are not performing.
We are living.
I am satisfied. And it is delicious.

We have been raised to fear the yes within ourselves, our deepest cravings.
—Audre Lorde

SENSUALITY

"You don't have to be nervous."

"I'm not."

I'm standing bedside, wearing black lingerie, feeling calm and confident. I'm taking up space. I've come a long way. I'm not sculpted. My body has not been nipped, tucked, or lifted. I am curvy. I am beautiful. I am beautiful, not because someone has deemed me so or because I have checked certain boxes, but just because I am. I am a woman who moves her body and enjoys red wine with her pasta. I stand here, proud of who I am, inviting my husband into my sensuality.

It hasn't always been this way. My capacity to access sensuality has complicated beginnings and even more complicated layers. For the last year, I've been exploring and trying to make sense of it—sensuality—this thing that has been shrouded in shame my entire life.

The year I first developed breasts and first wore a bra was the same year a classmate first groped me in the hallway. I was eight. I was mortified and humiliated. This young boy with a bowl haircut and a tucked-in shirt started a chain of events that has cascaded through my life and is still with me today. Our young selves are so sweet and innocent, and when we get blindsided, it often sets us down an undesirable and hurtful path.

Right then . . . in front of my 3rd-grade classroom door . . . without having the language for it . . . I internalized that my own body threatened my safety. I knew I had an extra responsibility that no other 8-year-old that I knew had: to keep myself safe. My parents felt it, too. They began to dress me in demure clothing and keep an extra close eye on my interactions with boys.

As I grew older, I started to have crushes. Feelings started bubbling up inside of me. Liking boys was entirely inconvenient for me, and it was complicated by what I already knew: my own body was dangerous. Getting attention was like playing with fire.

The first time a boy kissed me, the sky opened. We

were flirting under his parent's carport as he grabbed my nine-year-old arms and went for it. He felt like a rebel to me, and it was thrilling. But I couldn't tell anyone. I thought I'd be labeled boy crazy. And I knew that boy-crazy girls were bad.

These gargantuan opposing feelings and perspectives were swirling around in my tiny heart and body, and engulfing that swirl was a fear of being bad. I desperately wanted to be a good girl—to be loved and accepted—so I buried the excitement. *I would not be boy crazy; I would not be bad.*

When big ideas like this swim around our minds with nowhere to go, they begin to confuse us. *Which viewpoint is correct? Which one should I believe?* We start to look for clues outside of ourselves. *What is acceptable? What can I admit? What do other people do?* None of my other friends were kissing in driveways, so I kept my experience all to myself.

I existed this way until I moved away from home and went to college. The distance helped me feel free. As a freshman, a young man I liked, Michael, also liked me. For the first time, I had access to my sensuality and excitement without fear of being bad. I was away from home. No one knew who I was. I didn't have an image to uphold. I could just be.

It was exhilarating, lust, hormones, novelty, space—it felt like driving a car just a little too fast. Soon, I learned Michael was also sleeping with other young women, which felt hurtful and belittling. I didn't know what to do with that. More swirl.

Michael was the first person I had been intimate with. *Wasn't this supposed to be it? Weren't we supposed to be together? In love?* I was in deep, and if I admitted it to anyone, I'd be bad. Dirty. Someone's whore. So, I kept it quiet.

When we don't have language for what we are feeling or experiencing, it prolongs the confusion and suffering and complicates matters.

A few years later, the next complicated layer fell—sexual assault. Over half of women in the U.S. have experienced sexual violence involving physical contact during their lifetimes.[1] Still, I didn't know that when I was sexually assaulted by two men of two different ethnicities in two different cities. Once while I was an undergraduate student and once while I was a graduate student. Both times, I thought it was my fault.

I convinced myself that I hadn't made good decisions and had gotten myself into dangerous situations. I thought I was the problem and that maybe I deserved it. In those moments, faced with the fear of a man's body coming at mine, it was easier to give away my body than to speak my truth. I tried to write the experiences off and convince myself I was fine. But I couldn't.

Growing up, I never knew where girls and young women could go to talk about any of this—about butterflies, about sex, about the warm feelings I had when a man I liked put his hand on the small of my back or when a man sexually assaulted me. I grew up in a culture and home where sexuality and attraction were avoided and mostly forbidden.

Growing up, I tumbled through experiences and feelings, having no one to tell me whether what I was experiencing was normal, okay, or legitimately dangerous. I figured it out on my own—or didn't figure it out, as it were. I thought my mom would never approve of any of my feelings or explorations, and if I mentioned them, I knew I'd be judged, punished, or cause a sense of worry or shame. *What daughter wants to disappoint their mother?* So, I held it all in.

But the sexual assaults were causing collateral damage, and I knew I had to get help. In desperation, I shared the experiences with my mom. In that moment, I hoped that she would see my hurt and help me, and somehow, I'd get to bypass the fact that I was sexual at all. When I spoke up, she was there for me. She was a mother who listened to her daughter. A woman who listened to a woman. I was so grateful that she didn't judge me but instead went into action mode and found me mental health support. I don't remember exactly what that mental health support was, but I do remember that my mom was there. That's what sticks with me to this day.

Still, these inconvenient truths continued to sit inside me—my sensuality and desires were risky. They could warm me, but they could also burn me. I resigned that I'd never be able to bring these parts of me together. They would have to stay compartmentalized. If I had only known then that desiring and wanting to be desired is normal and part of the human experience.

Because I didn't want to be known as a slut, any enjoyable sex I had was done in obscurity. I would enjoy myself the most with men who resided on the outskirts of my life. There were the Saturday night types of men and the Sunday family brunch types of men. I worked hard to keep those parts of my life and my identity seperate.

In my early thirties, I fell in love with my then-boyfriend and now husband, Anthony. Part of it was because he was respectful, loving, and safe. And part of it was because he was fun and handsome and gave me butterflies. He felt like a Saturday night through Sunday morning man. His sense of wholeness helped me ease into my own.

For our honeymoon in 2013, I packed lacy black lingerie, because that's what new wives do. But as I walked out of the hotel bathroom, I short-circuited, fell into Anthony's arms, and cried. In many ways, my performative good girl and bad sensual girl compartments were together and being seen by someone—for the very first time. I couldn't take it. The part of me that hid in the darkness came out, and the light was too much.

It took 10 years of a loving marriage, physical safety, and compassion to get to where I could put on that same black honeymoon lingerie and stand proud.

My thirties were a quest for wholeness. Some of my wholeness was claimed by deconstructing cultural and religious conditioning, some of my wholeness was claimed with the help of therapy, and some was claimed by my learning to inhabit my own body.

I began to pay attention to power dynamics and

started to read and study the waves of feminists and wise women who came before me to offer me *even this*. I stopped listening to religious voices that had filled me with shame and started drinking wisdom from the cups of Maya Angelou, Tarana Burke, Isabel Allende, Jane Fonda, Elise Loehen, Hillary McBride, Cheryl Strayed, Maureen Murdock, and Audre Lorde. Their voices, courageous truths, and lives helped to teach me that I was not dishonorable in my wholeness, but rather my wholeness was to be appreciated and honored. Those women, among others, taught me to look at my own life through a different lens.

I began to examine sexual shame and purity culture and notice its place in my life. I began to look at how, from a young age, girls are taught that their sensuality is dirty and that they are better when they don't give into their impure thoughts or urges.

Where I once thought sexual harassment was just the price I paid for being a woman, I realized that sexual harassment is not the price I pay for being a woman, it's the price I pay for the poor choices of men.

These cultural expectations, aspirations, norms, and judgments are limiting at best and poisonous at worst. And when trauma is layered on top of that, our insides can feel impossible to understand, sit with, or accept.

I began to see that it is my turn, as a woman, to carry the torch; to blaze the way even farther so that my daughters are free to expand and to be whole and to not have to play into clichés and conditioning. It took a decade for me to acknowledge my complicated layers—to be curious about them and reconcile them. It's taken me 10 years to feel safe enough to admit and show that side of myself: to appreciate it, and to integrate.

Today, I am not a martyr.

Today I am all of me, all at once, all the time.

I am not too much, I am whole. I am a powerful woman making a *gentle return* to herself. The closer to whole I get, the more powerful I am.

Inhabiting my body has looked like a jiu-jitsu class—feeling my physical and creative power, and dancing with friends. Getting to know my body has looked like gazing at it naked and welcoming it instead of criticizing it. It looks like uncovering the truth about social media platforms, filters, and companies like Victoria's Secret that pedestalize supermodel beauty but are run by men I don't respect.

Stepping into my sensuality has looked like flirting

with my husband in the middle of the day, admitting to wanting sex, and letting myself be turned on by the sun's warmth on my skin.

Unraveling the shame surrounding my sensuality has been uncomfortable and has given me access to a part of myself I never thought I'd be able to embrace. I do like to play and explore. I do get turned on. It's okay to feel sexual pleasure.

I'm not a bad girl. I'm not a good girl. I am a woman.

We are not bad girls. We are not good girls. We are women.

"You don't have to be nervous."

"I'm not."

Although the world is full of suffering, it is also full of the overcoming of it.
—Helen Keller

THE UNFOLDING

I was none the wiser. I had a brand new 6-month-old daughter. I was trying to fit my new life into my old life. I wanted to *get back to myself.* I went to the gym, returning to my old standards of joy: weights and a treadmill.

Only this time, my old standards weren't enough. I'd press play on my songs—with their up-tempo pace—but each song fell flat. No motivation. My workout felt like I was just going through the motions. I felt lonely and bored. There was no mistaking it, I had lost touch with my joy.

Joy has always been like this for me—an elusive, moving target. It seems to shift and morph right before my eyes, even as it calls me forth into a new self. At each stage of my life, it reveals new meanings and nuances, like an old friend who I am constantly getting to know better. And each time, my new life somehow contains all the pieces of my old life, but never in the same way. Each time I must rediscover what unlocks my joy—like a familiar rose unfolding in a new morning.

I had long done this dance with joy and her likenesses of great pleasure, delight, euphoria, thrill, and happiness. Always cat and mouse. Always yes and no.

I can remember, as a young girl, hiding from joy, as I watched my classmates play and goof off. Instead of it inspiring me, joy did the opposite—it frightened me. I wondered, *how can they put themselves out there like that?* I feared being teased. I didn't want to get it wrong.

Growing up, I tried to distance myself from joy, figuring that if I wasn't trying to be joyful, I wouldn't be foolish. I thought being silly and being joyful were one and the same. So, I closed up. My young mind created a story that I didn't have time to be silly or joyful because I was working so hard. For me, being silly and letting loose with total abandon was for people who were not focused on accomplishing their goals. In my young mind, I couldn't be taken seriously while also being completely free, spirited, and a child.

I presented like a normal kid. I played drums in the marching band. I was invited to birthday parties, and I performed in jazz recitals. Yet even as an active participant, I always felt like an outsider looking in, barely belonging. I rarely let anyone see the real me. That would be way too vulnerable.

In college, I began to drink alcohol, and discovered what I would consider something fun. I would initiate conversations, let loose, and laugh louder. Cocktails lowered my inhibitions. But the fun was fleeting. The joys of alcohol weren't truly mine to own or enjoy.

Later in life, I started to chase the heady rush of exhilaration. Big events. Big risks. I would choose to put myself in situations where I'd feel an adrenaline rush; electricity pulsating through my veins. But there was real danger, and always a painful crash.

So, I turned to healthy challenges, seeking joy in feelings of triumph. Tough Mudders, Spartan races, marathons, rock climbing, skydiving, and even rappelling down a 32-story building. Each time I completed something new, my confidence would rise.

Over time, an unfamiliar feeling started to bubble up alongside exhilaration. *Was it . . . Could it be . . . Joy!*

I was around 30 years old when I finally found joy.

Throughout my life I had found things that let me feel silly and lighthearted, happy, exhilarated, or fun, but I had never quite learned how to be truly joyful.

It was overwhelming.

Something about pushing myself in new ways had unlocked my heart, not because I was winning; but because I had learned how to trust myself without judgment. I had learned how to unfold from within. I had learned how to just be.

And then, just as quickly as I realized the true nature of joy, it slipped from my fingers in the whirlpool of change.

I became a mother, and the combination of a massive identity shift, birth trauma, and postpartum depression drained all joy from my body. Many of the ways I had relied on to unfold and experience joy were not available to me anymore. Those healthy challenges were now memories. And, weights and a treadmill were no longer enough.

Would I ever feel silly, happy, exhilarated, or joyful again? I wasn't sure.

New life has a way of redefining the needs of our hearts.

One day, while at the gym, I saw women begin to filter into the group class studio, and I got curious. *What class was about to start?* I coyly walked to the studio door and ran my finger across the day's class schedule page. *11:00 a.m.—dance fitness. That sounds corny*, I thought, my smugness hiding my interest and budding fear. Instead of going in, I kept the dance room in my line of sight as I continued my workout.

I listened as the instructor turned up the music. I could feel the bass coming through the studio windows. The women were dancing. There was choreography, and they were into it! They were lost in the music, rhythm, and their bodies. I found myself thinking, *I want to be a part of that.* The very thing I labeled corny was the same thing giving me goosebumps.

The next day I walked into class, set my gym bag to the side, and found my spot in the back row. *What's the worst that could happen?*

Those first few classes were tricky. My feet weren't used to moving so fast, my hips weren't used to shaking, and I wasn't very good. But it didn't matter. I felt good.

I quickly became a dance enthusiast. Somehow, I could feel that every woman was there to feel good, which created so much space for possibility. No one was there to compete or judge. Everyone was there just to feel good. I was in love with the feeling, and with the experience.

I felt happy, silly, exhilarated, and joyful.
It was a complete unfolding of my spirit.

Something about sharing space with other women who, too, were letting loose felt so safe to me. I allowed myself to unfurl, like an orchid happy with its environment. A group of women, most of whom I didn't know, dancing in sync to beats; each one of us really going for it on a weekday, became its own kind of spiritual experience for me.

We jiggled and jumped, and I moved my body in weird, silly ways. I shook my booty, clapped, and swiveled my hips. With each song I could feel the heaviness of forcing myself to take myself seriously—a weighted personal protection—start to lift. For one hour a day, I entered a group fitness studio, gave my all to the music, left the seriousness on the hardwood floor, and walked out with joy in my heart. I was so grateful.

Joy and I had found each other. Again. I am always amazed at how the divine mystery of life unfolds. Whenever we think we have arrived at our final destination, another layer begins to unfold.

Of course, one exercise class is not enough. My old life was never able to fit neatly into my new life. But the experience of letting go and dancing for an hour a day with women pointed me in the direction of my new self, and it reminded me joy is always possible. That keeps me going.

After becoming a mom, I still needed time, therapy, antidepressants, and support to help recalibrate a life that felt good to me. It took time, but I created it.

It wasn't until after I had settled into my new rhythm that I stumbled on yet another, more expansive, accessible, and sustainable way to experience joy. It had nothing to do with vices, challenges, accomplishments, or seriousness.

I could access joy by letting go. I could access it by allowing myself to be in fullness, no matter whose gaze I was in. Joy is always there, ready to unfold, just waiting for me to recognize it.

As a new mom, I learned again how to experience joy, how to be present and unfurl my tight, protective petals during big and small moments. I find joy in the twinkle of my daughter's eyes. I find joy in a calm ocean, and in biting into a sweet piece of watermelon. I learned how to release and experience joy dancing with my girls, laughing with my husband, sharing chips and salsa with a girlfriend, and listening to Celia Cruz classics while I wash the dishes.

Many things demand our attention: hobbies, responsibilities as citizens of our neighborhoods and communities, and jobs. All sorts of things say, "This is the way. You must do this." And while many of those things are important and valid, joy is equally essential.

It takes courage to feel joy, to unfold and expose ourselves.
It takes courage to let it in and let it dance inside us.
Joy can live there, in our hearts, with everything else. Simultaneously.
Joy isn't a luxury.
Joy is a necessity.

One day, not long ago, my experience of joy expanded, again.

I was dropping off Luciana at her weekly dance class and she was timid and teary. While clutching her teddy bear, she looked at me and said, "I'm going to miss you. I'm sad." In a moment of God's grace, I responded, "Want to know a secret? We can miss someone and be happy at the same time."

"We can?"
"Sure, we can!"

And there it was, a new layer of joy unfolding in not just my life, but in the life of my daughter.

Emotions are layered and complex. There are no clean lines, and that's okay. Life will bring us sad events and sad moments, but life itself does not have to be sad. There is no need to close up. There will be many joyful moments, too.

We must permit ourselves to feel joy alongside other emotions.

What I have learned is that joy will arrive and unfold in many ways and forms throughout the course of our lives. Our moments of unfolding will be layered with lightness, brightness, excitement, peace, gratitude, and happiness.

Joy isn't scarce, it's abundant, and regenerative.

It can be found everywhere, when we allow ourselves to see it. Sometimes it will be just a flicker, other times it will last for hours.

I still go to my exercise class and dance my heart out every chance I get, but I also know that joy will not always be found in the same room or in the same way. It changes as we change. And in the change, joy serves as a *gentle return*. It waits for us in dance class, in laughter, and in a warm embrace. It opens us up when we learn new skills, explore new parts of our city, or cook a meal with our family. It appears and helps us unfold when we serve others, or in that moment when we catch ourselves laughing together around a campfire.

As a mother and a woman, I know that joy will always be available to me in all its forms, and it will always call me, back to myself and forth into my new heart.

Joy will take every opportunity to unfold,
and when we can embody joy,
it will show us the way forward, sustain us through hardship,
and illuminate us from the inside out.

Just because it has not happened
Does not mean it cannot happen.
Beauty creates her own chances.
—Scott Andrew James

———————

KARAOKE

"Everyone, get your costumes on," I say gleefully. With full bellies, we all scurry to our closets, assembling our best talent show outfits. We leave the Thanksgiving dinner clean up for later . . . better for dessert grazing and better to enjoy the moment.

I set up our family's karaoke machine in the living room and start untangling the microphones. Our girls are 8 and 5, and like their mother, they've never met a mic they didn't like. For me, a microphone means possibility. And although I've always loved wielding a mic, it took me years to actually admit it. I was afraid of being teased and being too much.

The words, *you're so full of yourself* still follow me decades later, threatening to define me. I often make a deal and play small. But not tonight. I'm with my daughters and my husband tonight, and those judgmental words don't exist in this home.

Anthony comes back sporting an old tuxedo complete with a red cummerbund and bowtie, and the flip-flops he wears during yard work. Our girls arrive—ready to perform—in costumes that are part punk rock, part mermaid—and I come ready to perform in a felt hat that wears me, a camel-colored duster, and cowboy boots.

These last six months, I have been feeling the bandages wrapped tightly around my personality begin to loosen. I've been letting loose more and more.

"Welcome to the first annual Holm talent show! Our first performance will be by Alexandra! Please welcome Alexandra to the stage!" We all cheer, and my first-born begins her routine, a combination of dance, gymnastics, and audacity. "I'm always up for a good audience," she giggles as she sees our eyes twinkle with wonder and delight.

"How does she do that?" I whisper to her dad as he captures the moment on a cellphone camera. He answers with a shoulder shrug to avoid interrupting her performance. "Bravo! Next up, Mama!"

When I was a young girl, I would get teased because

my singing voice was so bad, so I stopped singing. I'd make light of my lack of ability and say I was tone-deaf. Too often, we reject ourselves first before anyone else has a chance to. When we do that, we think we are guarding the pain of it all, but we end up getting hurt anyway. It was inconvenient that I liked music, and I liked to sing. I'd force myself to settle for muttering lyrics or humming in the car. I adapted to the bullying and teasing by being serious; if I was serious, I would weed myself out. "Catia won't want to play." Another way of rejecting myself before anyone else could.

I didn't fit in, so rather than trying to fit in and failing, rather than focusing on friendships and matters of youth, I focused on matters of the mind—a predictable path where rejection wasn't a threat.

Tonight, I walk up to the stage, which on any other day is the living room rug, two feet from the karaoke machine. I pick up a mic, find my song, and open my mouth.

I can hear my mousy voice hitting the mic, so I bring the mic closer. I'm reading lyrics and trying to stay on key as my hips sway my duster from left to right.

My kids have seen me be me.

Pleasant and unpleasant.
Raw and polished.
Silly and serious.

They are so unaffected by cultural standards and expectations. They just are. They know mom is loud and sometimes farts in their bedroom and laughs as she walks away. Mom destroys cupcakes, listens to salsa, and sometimes leaves the kitchen a mess.

In theory and practice, I know I can be myself around my husband, and while he has heard me sing, he has never heard me *really try to sing*. Ten years together and some parts of my spirit are still under wraps.

Sometimes the people we are closest to don't know all of who we are. Sometimes we perform the most in the most intimate areas of our lives. Sometimes we keep parts of ourselves hidden even from the people we love the most. But today, I want to be fully known.

As I sing, I start jumping up and down in my cowboy boots. Three jumps in, I remember that rock stars can really make it look easy. Between breaths, I decide it'll be a good performance without jumping. I keep going—off-key—singing, and I feel my face flush. I realize I'm embarrassed because my husband is watching this new part of me. I keep going, singing in earnest.

I scan the room, and my girls are clapping and singing; they've seen this before. My husband is wide-eyed and smiling. He is moving to the beat, and I can tell by the sweetness in his eyes and grin that he isn't going to laugh at me or give one note on my performance and that maybe he is into it—into *me being into something*.

I keep singing with Florence and the Machine, "You can't carry it with you if you want to survive." I close my eyes, and my voice projects into the mic. I decide to try. I decide to try even though I will suck. I choose not to hold back. My soft Mexican hips sway side to side, my husband is recording me—and I'm not combusting into flames. I am me; I am okay. I sing all four minutes and thirty seconds. It is glorious.

I put the mic down, curtsy, and welcome our youngest daughter to the stage. I take my place on the couch, cotton-mouthed, my heart pounding.

It doesn't look like anything has changed. Five minutes ago, I was sitting in my living room with my kids and my husband, planning for a second helping of pumpkin pie, and while that's still true, I've since changed. My spirit has tasted real air. I stood in the awkwardness of my whole self. I uncovered a part of myself that had been hiding for so long, and I had fun doing it.

My youngest daughter, Luciana, takes the stage for her song, "Worth It." She glows as she is part mermaid and part punk rocker. Her sister counts her in with drumsticks and a snare drum, and Luciana takes it away. "Give it to me. I'm worth it!" She sings with a knowing, makes eye contact with her audience, and works the room. I am alive with contentment.

Being raw is risky. *Will they laugh? Will they judge? Will I recover? Will I implode from embarrassment?* Our insides can monumentally shift, and everything around us can remain, but how we see and experience the situation changes. We can take a leap, change our perspective, or release a hurt and walk around seemingly the same, but nowhere close to where we started.

I am grateful for this night in our living room. We gathered with full bellies and full hearts and chose to share our full selves. We chose to show each other our creative, homemade costumes and to sing with our real voices. We chose to show up and trust each other. And we discovered parts of each other—and ourselves—that we didn't even know needed a breath of fresh air.

I think about how rare, beautiful, brave, and awkward it is to show all the different parts of ourselves that live within us. I think about what it means for each of us to be our whole self. Maybe that's the talent we're really portraying this Thanksgiving, being whole.

Tonight, we were not worried about being too much. We were full of ourselves—full of our true, whole selves. And for that, I am truly thankful.

TIME TO RETURN

Sometimes you will feel sad and hurt. Sometimes, there will be times when you want to cry and disappear because you don't like how things are going. This is all okay. This is all normal. It happens to all of us.

Before I gave birth, people told me I would forget about the pain once the baby arrived. They said, "You won't even remember how much it hurt once you see her sweet face." I thought they were crazy. *How could they forget the pain of a human body leaving their human body?*

And yet, a few weeks into being a new mother, when I looked back at the picture taken by our doula moments after Alexandra was born, I saw the anguish on my face, the fibrous umbilical cord, my sweaty legs high up in stirrups, and blood everywhere. I thought, *I know it was brutal, but I don't remember it that well.*

Now I know that forgetting is a kindness offered by our brain. The trauma of childbirth is so much to bear that the brain tucks away the pain and instead washes us in oxytocin. Now I hardly remember the pain. I know it happened, I know I went through it, but the pain isn't alive—it's been alchemized.

Giving birth made me an entirely different woman. Pregnancy, labor, and new motherhood forced me to be introspective—to shed superficial identities I was holding onto. Giving birth made me become stronger. Much stronger. Who I was before pregnancy, labor, and motherhood didn't hold a candle to who I was after. And so, the lens through which I viewed things changed. I no longer needed the perspective of the single 28-year-old, I needed to experience the perspective of a 31-year-old woman, mother, and wife.

Sometimes people will be mean to you for no reason, or you will try out for something and fall short, or you will love someone, and they won't love you back. These things happen, and they can feel anywhere from annoying to gut-wrenching.

When these things happen, my heart will break with yours. And as much as I would like to shield you from discomfort or pain, I know these are the moments in which you will learn who you are.

In March 2020, the world came to a screeching halt. A deadly and wide-sweeping airborne novel coronavirus caused a global pandemic. The world felt unsafe, and leaving the house was always a risk for our family. We pulled our girls out of school, Anthony stopped traveling for work, we stopped shopping at stores, and public parks shut down. Families stopped seeing families, birthday parties morphed into drive-by parades, and we stayed home. Congregating was risky, so people sheltered in their homes to keep safe.

As the pandemic began, Anthony got very sick, and we weren't sure if it was the virus or something else; we had to be extra careful. Our house dynamics shifted in the first weeks during the global shutdown. Anthony quarantined in one room of the house, never leaving for fear of infecting us. No one was allowed in or out of our home, and we did not socialize with anyone. We took every precaution to keep safe. When Anthony got sick it was extra hard. Every day, I was a mom, wife, nurse, housekeeper, teacher, employee, and coach.

My days were packed trying to give our girls a sense of normalcy and joy, fearing that the world shutting down would alter them forever. I wonder if they will remember anything at all.

As Anthony's illness got worse, we decided he needed to go to the emergency room. But since we didn't know if he was infected with the virus, he couldn't hug or kiss us as he left our house for the hospital. On his way out the door, he waved goodbye. "We love you." "I love you, and I'll be back."

But he and I knew that he was not sure. He and I knew that the unspoken truth was—I love you, I love the girls, take good care of them if anything happens . . .

Our daughters waved goodbye and went back to watching television, and I immediately went to Luciana's bedroom and sobbed. I sat in a tiny pink chair and huddled over my knees, bellowing, and sobbing in despair. *Please, God, heal Anthony and give him strength.*

And as gut-wrenching as it was saying goodbye to my beloved, and even as I write this in the three years since, that worry sits differently in my heart and mind because that experience changed me. I have been through it.

These moments of heartbreak and sadness feel terrible, and we all want them to disappear.

But even painful moments can eventually be
meaningful:
The opportunity to go inward.
The opportunity to get still, reflect, and listen.

Why did this happen?
What can I learn from this situation?
What can I do differently next time?
What is the universe trying to communicate?
What are my strengths?
What is going well?
What can come of this?

The world will entice you with food, sex, drugs, new
clothes, relationships, and work—all things that
point outward from your center. These things will
promise fulfillment, joy, the promise of less stress,
easing or even removing your hurt. But know this,
no arrow pointing outward will ever truly deliver.

The answer will always be to go deeper into your
center, deeper into your well of grace and kindness,
deeper into your connection with God.

The answer will always be in the going through.

How can you rise, change, adjust, change perspective, and grow? Can you clarify what you want and

what experiences you want? How can you identify more deeply with the person you want to become?

Every single heartbreak can eventually be perceived as a gift, an opportunity for things to crystallize. The clearer you are about who you are and what you want, the more joy you will attract and embody.

You arrived full of wisdom and grace, and love. Steward your spirits and give yourself the environment and the space to expand as far and as wide as you desire.

There is no answer on the outside. All the answers rest within you. You are divine, magic, and you already know what to do.

Situations can seem intense, dire, unfair, and tragic—and then later, after you have walked through it, your perspective shifts because your vantage point is different.

You will acquire new strengths, learn to trust yourself in new ways, lean into God more, and shed more untruths. And then, you'll realize that you are one of those women who live to tell their story with a miraculous sense of kindness in their eyes and grounding in their being. Assuredly, tough times will come, but you will make it through.

One day you will realize that,

you are the kind of woman who can
make a *gentle return* to herself

you are the kind of woman who can
embrace her wholeness and her goodness

you are the kind of woman who can
embody fulfillment, pleasure, and worth

you are the kind of woman who can
make the world a better place just by being herself.

We can walk together.

Shall we?

ACKNOWLEDGMENTS

Anthony, your love has allowed me to grow and explore parts of myself I never thought possible. You are a dream. I am so proud to be married to you. My heart skips a beat when I see you walk across a room. I love our life together, and I'm grateful for you every day.

Luciana, my sweet girl. You are fun and cuddly and great at Uno. I love our belly-to-belly hugs, and I love being your mama. You are my sunshine.

Alexandra, my darling girl. You are soulful and wise and great at back flips. I love hearing you sing and dancing with you in the kitchen. I love being your mama. The world is lucky to have you.

Mom, I love you dearly. You are one of my life's greatest treasures. Thank you for being the best mom I could hope for, even now—as I turn 40. I love you.

Dad, thank you for believing in me and giving me the gift of stability and love. I am still in awe and impressed at how well you loved me and continue to. I love you. I believe in you, too.

Scott, thank you for saying yes and for your presence. I love working together.

Sheila, thank you for your art! I couldn't be happier working together.

Comads, thank you for your multiple decade-long friendship. You are a blessing in my life. I hope we'll always be two sassy gals. And thank you for helping this book be the best it could be. *Nicky*, finding you was a gift from God. I love you. *Tracy*, there's no one I'd rather talk to about raising girls and being a wife and mom with. You're such a good friend. *Grace*, your spirit helps me live into the fullness of my own. Thank you. *Ashley*, I am so proud of you. I'm so glad we are family. *Gabby*, thank you for all your love; I am grateful for you.

And to you, the reader, thank you for holding my story close. These stories, these seminal moments in my life, are so profoundly intimate, as yours are. I am grateful for your compassion, trust, and connection with my writing. I pray that my work lights the possibility inside your heart and spirit.

BIBLIOGRAPHY

1 (2022). Fast Facts: Preventing Sexual Violence. https://www
   .cdc.gov/violenceprevention/sexualviolence/fastfact.html

ABOUT THE AUTHOR

Catia Hernández Holm is a dedicated Marriage and Family Coach and a Certified Conscious Parenting Coach with global reach. Her gifts of empathy and compassion, combined with her hope-giving spirit, empower women and families worldwide to step into the best version of themselves. Through her guidance, they discover and celebrate their unique gifts, propelling them toward more fulfilling and meaningful lives.

Catia's captivating TEDx talk, "Choose Joy or Die," has inspired countless viewers, while her debut book, "The Courage to Become," achieved instant acclaim. She has been widely featured on ABC, CBS, NBC, and the Austin American Statesman.

In 2024, Catia will be a licensed marriage and family therapist working at the intersection of intergenerational trauma, mindfulness, and somatic processing within a systems framework.

Catia lives in the Texas Hill Country with her family.

Connect with Catia:

CATIAHOLM.COM

IN THE SHADOW OF THE ROCKS

IN THE SHADOW OF THE ROCKS

ARCHAEOLOGY OF THE CHIMNEY ROCK DISTRICT
IN SOUTHERN COLORADO

Florence C. Lister

THE HERALD PRESS
Durango   Colorado

COVER DESIGN
Roy Paul
BASED ON PHOTOGRAPHS
courtesy of
Jean Carson
and
United States Forest Service

Originally published by the University Press of Colorado
in cooperation with
San Juan Mountain Association
and the
Amoco Foundation.

Library of Congress Cataloging in Publication Data

Lister, Florence Cline.
    In the shadow of the rocks: archaeology of the Chimney Rock District in
    southern Colorado / Florence C. Lister.
        p.   cm.
    Includes bibliographical references and index.
    ISBN 1-887805-02-8   (acid-free paper)
    1. Pueblo Indians—Antiquities. 2. Indians of North America—Colo-
    rado—Chimney Rock Region (Archuleta County)—Antiquities. 3. Chim-
    ney RockRegion (Archuleta County, Colo.)—Antiquities. 4. Colorado—
    Antiquities.
    1. Title.
    E99.P9L518 1997
    978.8'32—dc20   97-066780
                                                            CIP

CONTENTS

Figures   vii

Preface   xi

PART I: THE PLACE

  1. La Piedra Parada   1

PART II: THE ARCHAEOLOGY

  2. The Diggers Arrive   9

  3. Anasazi Under Water   43

       Paleo-Indian, Archaic Periods   46

       Los Pinos Phase   47

       Sambrito Phase   53

       Rosa Phase   59

       Piedra Phase   64

       Arboles Phase   67

       Anasazi Upriver   68

       Anasazi Exposed   70

  4. Anasazi in the Backwater   75

PART III: EPILOGUE

  5. The Chimney Rock District to 1900   113

Selected References   131

Index   135

FIGURES

1.	Regional map of upper San Juan district	2
2.	State Historical and Natural History Society field camp	14
3.	Ground plan of Chimney Rock pueblo, 1921	16
4.	Shell pendant	17
5.	Ground plan of Harlan ranch site	19
6.	Mountain sheep vessel	24
7.	Chimney Rock pueblo, 1922	25
8.	Duck-shaped jar	26
9.	Frank H. H. Roberts, Jr.	28
10.	Roberts camp, 1923	29
11.	Ruin on Stollsteimer Mesa	32
12.	"Plaza Grande" site	33
13.	Terrace site, Chimney Rock cuesta	34
14.	Tower site, Chimney Rock cuesta	35
15.	Pueblo I village, Stollsteimer Mesa	36
16.	Jacal house type, Stollsteimer Mesa	37
17.	Pottery from Stollsteimer Mesa sites	39
18.	Pottery from Stollsteimer Mesa sites	40
19.	Navajo Reservoir map	44
20.	Twin War Gods pictograph	45
21.	Albino Village pithouse	49
22.	Pithouse type	50
23.	Sambrito Village, 1960	53
24.	Sambrito Village pithouse	54

25. Sambrito Phase cists   56
26. Sambrito Phase pottery   57
27. Sanchez Site excavations   61
28. Cists at Oven Site, 1989   71
29. Close-up of cist, Oven Site   72
30. Chimney Rock pueblo before stabilization   76
31. Chimney Rock pueblo before stabilization   77
32. Excavations at Chimney Rock pueblo, 1970   78
33. West kiva, Chimney Rock pueblo   79
34. Stabilized walls, Chimney Rock pueblo   80
35. Trail from Chimney Rock pueblo   81
36. Site 5AA92, Chimney Rock mesa   82
37. View from Chimney Rock mesa   83
38. Unexcavated sites, terraces of Chimney Rock mesa   84
39. Payan Corrugated jar   85
40. Village clusters, Chimney Rock Archeological Area   87
41. Site 5AA88, Chimney Rock mesa   89
42. Room at Site 5AA88   90
43. Ground plan of Site 5AA88   91
44. Milling bins, Site 5AA88   92
45. Grinding Stones   92
46. Ground plan of Parking Lot Site   93
47. Parking Lot Site after excavation   94
48. Photographing Parking Lot Site   95
49. Ground plan of Great Kiva, Site 5AA88   96
50. Great Kiva after excavation   97
51. Great Kiva after stabilization   97
52. Chimney Rock pueblo (Site 5AA83) after excavation   99
53. Chaco roads   101

54. Securing tree-ring specimens, Chimney Rock pueblo   102
55. Feather holder   107
56. Forked-stick hogan   117
57. European objects from Pueblo refugee sites   118
58. Pueblo refugee site   119
59. Hispanic family moving to southern Colorado   126
60. Ute and buggy   127
61. Ute house   127
62. Penitente rites   128
63. Utes dipping sheep   129

PREFACE

In 1970, 3,160 acres of the Pagosa district of the San Juan National Forest were set aside as the Chimney Rock Archeological Area, making it the largest high-mountain archaeological zone in the national forest system. It is situated within the boundaries of the Southern Ute Indian Reservation and is a special precinct to these Native Americans. Also in 1970, a 960-acre block of land containing the greatest concentration of prehistoric remains in the national forest system was placed on the National Register of Historic Places. Subsequently, an intensive National Park Service/University of New Mexico research project in Chaco Canyon National Monument underscored the connection of the major Chimney Rock site to a pan–San Juan Basin Chacoan system, and legislation was put before Congress to add the Chimney Rock Archeological Area to the Chaco Archeological Protection Site System. These various designations are part of long-term programs to protect the antiquities and make them available to the public through development of visitor facilities and understandable through interpretive materials.

The southern base of the pinnacles of Companion and Chimney rocks has the added value of being an aerie of peregrine falcons. These birds of prey typically nest at the top of high talus slopes having ledges with gravel or soil into which depressions for eggs can be scraped. The protection of this endangered species and its habitat is a second mission incorporated into the area's management.

This publication necessarily goes beyond the territory immediately surrounding Chimney Rock in order to establish the cultural background from which the local expression evolved and to carry interpretation through to modern historic occupations. Two thousand years of human history are represented. I needed the aid of many people in presenting this long continuum. Thanks are extended to Curtis Schaafsma, Louise Stiver, Rosemary Talley, and Willow Powers, Museum of

New Mexico; Helen Pustmeuller, Department of Anthropology, University of Denver; Katherine Kane, Anne Bond, and Mary Sullivan, Colorado Historical Society; Robert McDaniel, Animas Valley Museum; Nancy Hammack, Complete Archaeological Service Associates; Charles H. Lange, formerly University of Northern Illinois; Gary Matlock and Tom McMurray, San Juan National Forest; Laurie Gruel, San Juan National Forest Association; John W. Sanders and Bob Snyder, San Juan Basin Archaeological Society. Some specimen photographs were taken by Gary G. Lister. Funding by the Amoco Foundation is gratefully acknowledged.

Most important to the temporal and cultural framework of this summary were the thorough technical reports on both the Navajo Reservoir and Chimney Rock areas by Frank W. Eddy, University of Colorado. In general, the reconstructions of the past presented here are his. However, in the years since Eddy's work, varying interpretations have been put forth, and they are included where germane. Thanks are also due Eddy for generous permission to use an assortment of unpublished field photographs.

This book should have been my husband's to write. On behalf of the University of Colorado, he negotiated the original agreements with the Southern Ute Indian Tribe and the San Juan National Forest to conduct archaeological surveys and excavations on their lands. When the San Juan National Forest Association and the San Juan Basin Archaeological Society decided to sponsor a synthesis for the interested public of the prehistoric human drama played out in the upper San Juan district, he agreed to do the job. But that was not to be.

Therefore, with the guidance of four valued family friends and distinguished regional archaeologists — David A. Breternitz, W. James Judge, Marcia Truell Newren, and R. Gwinn Vivian — I have endeavored to fulfill this commitment. With such expertise at hand, any shortcomings in the text obviously are my sole responsibility.

So this book is for you, Robert H. Lister (1915–1990): educator, digger, administrator, lecturer, father, and my love.

FLORENCE C. LISTER
Mancos, Colorado

PART I
THE PLACE

1

LA PIEDRA PARADA

Two stone pinnacles loom side by side on an elevated promontory overlooking the head of the Piedra River valley in south central Colorado. They scratch the hard blue sky for rain and snow, often are obscured by swirling cloud banks, and at times seem to stand defiant before brilliant bolts of summer lightning that rip the firmament. Behind them tower the San Juan Mountains, evergreen on lower slopes, bald and formidable above, and comprising an arm of the massif that diverts continental waters east and west. At their feet to the south sweeps a variegated panorama of broken ramparts and tablelands stiffly folding down to the semidesert lands embracing an interior basin, through which slices the San Juan River, major tributary to the upper Colorado River. At a distance the small Piedra, the easternmost substantial stream of the secondary network, meanders in quiet counterpoint through a shallow U-shaped depression and bordering floodplains on its way from the snowmelt of the Rockies to its merger with the San Juan. Their former confluence now is blocked by the impounded waters of the man-made Navajo Reservoir. The view to the west is obstructed by tiers of cliffs and high blue mesas that level down to the Pine River valley. To the east rises a barricade of successive ranges, each reaching greater heights and structural complexity. Here, where the two stony pinnacles eternally stand guard, the expansive plateau of the northern Southwest finally is boxed in.

Eighteenth-century Spaniards called the spires *La Piedra Parada*, the upright or standing rock. Less eloquently, nineteenth-century Americans referred to them as Chimney Rock, one of many natural monuments in the West with the identical name. Strangely, both terms were

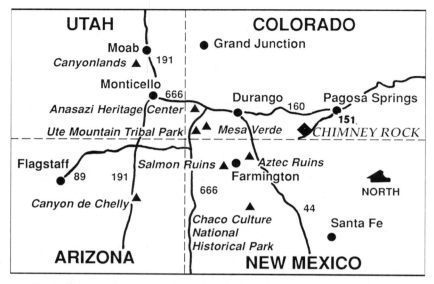

Regional map of upper San Juan district showing location of the Chimney Rock Archeological Area.

used in the singular, which may reflect the fact that just one of the pillars is immediately apparent when seen straight on from east or west. Lower in height, greater in mass, and with less pleasing contours, the westerly one remained anonymous until an archaeologist alluded to it in the 1920s as the companion to the more spectacular adjacent Chimney Rock. Henceforth, the unnamed tower had an identity: Companion Rock.

Although the various Native American names for these stelae of nature are not known, assuredly the columns were recognized by the aborigines as landmarks having possible mythological significance. Modern Pueblo Indians generally consider such unique physiographic features to be representations of certain deities or spirits. If their predecessors had similar animistic beliefs, the rare pair of dominant shafts of stone rising more than a thousand feet above the nearby valley floor may have been regarded as the earthly symbols of the Twin War Gods, now prominent figures in the religious pantheon of the Pueblos. Believers regard them as offspring of the Sun God, born at the time of creation;

in some versions of the legendary accounts they built mountains and in others merely lived there. One of their attributes is the ability to turn themselves or their antagonists into stone. As prominent mountains and natural stone columns are both present in this locale, the attribution seems reasonable. However, if Chimney Rock and its companion were indeed viewed as sacred embodiments of the Twin War Gods, the prehistoric shrine we would expect to find in a cairn of rocks at their base with offerings of miniature bows and arrows, war clubs, shields, or prayer plumes placed on it has been stolen by time.

In geological terms, Chimney and Companion rocks are dramatic survivors of an inexorable process of erosion that for eons has been wearing down the Colorado Plateau and carrying it grain by grain to western waters. The two spires are unstable remnants of a relatively modest layer of tawny bedded rock, now called Pictured Cliff sandstone, that was deposited beneath an ancient inland sea. Blocky chunks of the chimneys themselves continue to break away and cascade down steep talus slopes formed by a soft, thick accumulation of dark Cretaceous shale. Plant matter and small organisms that fell into the coalescing sandstone stratum became fossilized and today, millions of years later, weather out of the matrix. Reported fossil patterns of ferns and sea shells confirm the passage of an earlier, warmer, watery episode. The geologic movement that crunched the mountain mass upward to the north simultaneously tilted the blocky landform on which the sandstone steeples would slowly be left freestanding. The rest of its more-or-less flat top sloped about ten degrees from northeast to southwest, with convoluted long inclines fanning down to the east and south and a precipitous escarpment exposed on the north face. In the Southwest the Spanish term *cuesta* is used to define such a formation, which in this instance appears as a final bridging platform between the lower San Juan Basin to the south and the lofty Rocky Mountains to the north. Waterways encircle the base of the cuesta at about 6,400 feet above sea level, whereas the cuesta surface reaches 7,600 feet, culminating in the Chimney Rock at an additional 300 feet. Along the north side an intermittent stream, Devil Creek, flows though a narrow defile separating the Chimney Rock mesa from the San Juan foothills and empties into the perennial Piedra River on the west. During the Pleistocene period, as the Piedra ate deeper into its channel, stepped terraces were left above it at the western end of the lower Chimney Rock mesa. To the east and south of the cuesta, another small Piedra tributary, Stollsteimer Creek, sluggishly moves southwest in years of sufficient moisture through a valley more expansive and open than that of Devil Creek.

The vegetational cover of the Piedra River district reflects increased elevation and precipitation as one moves the twenty miles upstream from the San Juan to the headgates formed by the Chimney Rock cuesta on the east and Petersen Mesa on the west, above which open space for horticulture is choked off. A riparian environment of willows, cotton-woods, rushes, and grasses marks the riverine bottom lands. Gravel-paved embankments lead up to sage- and brush-covered silt benches. Occasional stands of scrub oak, piñon, and juniper become thicker near the jagged mountain wall. A reversal of the usual life-zone pattern occurs at the towering Chimney Rock mesa: here, a relic yellow pine forest grows on lower southeastern slopes, while piñon and juniper trees stand on higher ground. This role-reversal is due to the cold winter air that drains into the narrow valleys. Steep clay ridges capped with sandstone and rocky cliff faces make up some of the exposed surfaces. However, before the introduction of sheep a hundred years ago, the area upriver was notable for billowing carpets of waist-high grasses and exuberantly blooming wildflowers that served to accentuate the valley's transitional linkage between the extremes of the denuded southern basin, where trees and other greenery are a novelty, and the aspen- and pine-forested northern mountains and lush but soggy alpine meadows.

Unpredictability characterized the regional climate. In modern times annual precipitation has averaged a little less than eighteen inches. Much of it comes with a vengeance. Often developing and then departing in the space of a few hours, violent summer thunderstorms boil the rivers with a supercharge of sediments as normally dry channels are flushed out bank to bank. Such rapid runoff reduces the amount of beneficial moisture reaching plant roots. At the opposite end of the spectrum are cyclical droughts, some lasting season after season. In winter, snows typically drift many feet deep. Accumulations on shaded slopes linger for months. At these times subzero temperatures are the norm. There are generally only three or four months a year when freezing does not occur. At best the average overall monthly temperature is in the forty-to-fifty degree range. But just as every July or August does not experience rain, not every January or February is completely snowbound.

Despite their picture-postcard beauty, these uplands of the Chimney Rock district, the northernmost outpost of the vast Colorado Plateau, have not sustained prosperous human occupation. The reasons range from topographic inhospitability to ecological stresses to historical circumstances. For the past millennium they have tested the mettle of a veritable parade of diverse cultures. But in the end they essentially remain, as they were in the beginning, the legendary province of the Twin War Gods.

PART II
THE ARCHAEOLOGY

2

THE DIGGERS ARRIVE

From the time of the first Spanish *entradas* in the last quarter of the eighteenth century, the upper San Juan Basin was known to contain scores of small ruins of unknown age and affiliation. It was not until the post–Civil War era, however, that they came to the attention of the public. Spanish-Americans out of New Mexico and Anglos from east of the Rockies began to traverse or settle the Chimney Rock district, noting numerous remains seemingly unrelated to the modern Utes then roaming the mesas and valleys. On an 1878 road survey trip into the San Juan Mountains, Lt. C.A.H. McCauley reported, "Long before the advent of the White man upon the continent [the San Juan River's] banks teemed with an unknown population of whose habits and mode of life history speaks. Only tradition is silent, with naught to aid the intelligent investigator save fragmentary pottery and the ruins of their dwellings" (Motter 1984, 45). Settlers clearing land for construction and gardens saw low knolls of stones, some encircling bowl-shaped depressions, that appeared to be collapsed houses. Bits of broken pottery, arrowheads, and stone flakes left from tool manufacture were strewn about. When the mounds were considered detrimental to farm development, they were leveled. A limited amount of leisure-time digging in the sites took place in order to secure "relics," particularly pottery vessels. However, the pottery and the sites themselves were so unprepossessing that the ruins generally were viewed merely as local curiosities. That fact, plus the very limited population moving into the Piedra Valley, helped to keep the bulk of the ruins from being vandalized.

According to an account in the *Pagosa Springs Sun* (February 28, 1930), one log house on a piece of land at the junction of Yellowjacket

9

and Squaw creeks three miles west of the Piedra Valley was "foundationed on the unfortunate ruins of the Aztecs." This article reflected a widespread belief in the late nineteenth century among farmers and ranchers that these evidences of an earlier occupation had been left behind by the Aztec Indians. That opinion originated in a popular book, *The History of the Conquest of Mexico* by William H. Prescott, which recounted an Aztec legend stating that their ancestors arrived in central Mexico after lengthy peregrinations from the far north. Without the benefit of archaeological research to prove otherwise, the association of the San Juan antiquities with the Mexican migrations was logical. (More scientific minds linked the vestiges of the past with the present-day Pueblo Indians.) However, the Aztecs did not emerge as an identifiable entity until several centuries after the upper San Juan area had been abandoned by its prehistoric occupants. The north from which the Aztecs came now is believed to have been the north central tableland of Mexico. In other words, the Aztecs were never on the San Juan, nor did they ever see the pair of dominant natural stone columns at the head of the Piedra drainage.

No scientific work was undertaken in the Piedra Valley until 1921. In that year J. A. Jeancon left the Smithsonian Institution to become curator of archaeology and ethnology at the State Historical and Natural History Society in Denver. He hit the ground running. With an avowed goal of getting Colorado involved in its own archaeology, in April he was off on an inspection trip to the southern part of the state, near Pagosa Springs. Based on photographs and observations of local parties, he believed there were many prehistoric sites in the vicinity.

At the beginning of the twenties, the growing ranks of Southwestern prehistorians had only sketchy ideas about the aboriginal societies that had developed on the Colorado Plateau and then inexplicably disappeared. Generally speaking, the large wrecked structures in open country and those hunkered down in alcoves in cliff faces had been the first to be studied because of their visibility, often spectacular settings, and the lure of large amounts of material goods found to be within them. The State Historical and Natural History Society had in its possession one of the collections the Wetherill brothers took from the Mesa Verde cliff dwellings in the 1890s. Stimulated by these finds, Richard Wetherill went on to participate in a four-year excavation at the huge bottomland settlement of Pueblo Bonito in Chaco Canyon. He and others of his time correctly thought that both the cliff dwellings and the ruins at Chaco represented a prehistoric climax to a long, entangled growth process that culminated in the modern Pueblo Indians of the Rio Grande, Zuni, and Hopi areas.

Between these two projects dealing with the supposedly final developmental stage on the Colorado Plateau, the Wetherills uncovered a manifestation of a different order. On the basis of the lack of architecture (other than storage cists scooped out of soft dirt alcove floors in escarpments of southeastern Utah) and primitive material arts (other than basketry taken from the alcove deposits), the diggers postulated that what they found represented an initial cultural evolutionary phase occurring centuries earlier than that of the cliff dwellings and perhaps involving a different aboriginal stock. The latter notion stemmed from a variant shape to skulls removed from burial sites. Richard Wetherill named this group of people the Basketmakers. Between these speculated earliest and latest expressions of aboriginal life on the Colorado Plateau, there remained a gaping void of perhaps many centuries.

At the exact time Jeancon took on his new job, a five-year excavation effort at a massive site at Aztec, New Mexico, sponsored by the prestigious American Museum of Natural History, was concluding amid a great deal of national press. That settlement on the Animas River just below the Colorado border obviously was erected by masons familiar with techniques used at Pueblo Bonito and was inhabited during the time the regional culture came to full flower. But elsewhere across southern Colorado and northern New Mexico, there were less pretentious remains of potential significance in filling the data gap between the beginning and end of the postulated prehistoric chronology. Jeancon made no bones about his desire to get himself and his new home institution in on the action.

An amateur archaeologist who was familiar with regional sites and had participated in some of the excavations at Aztec Ruins, J. S. Palmer, guided Jeancon to a locality that was densely occupied prehistorically. That was the Chimney Rock cuesta. As the men reached the upper slopes of the mesa, they met a series of craterlike pits, obviously man-made, rounded by massive stones held in place by mud mortar. These pits crowded one after another up the steep edges of the mesa. As the explorers ascended a ridge no more than twelve feet wide pointing toward the base of the pinnacles, they crossed what appeared to be portions of one small room that lay directly in their trail. Higher up, where the mesa flattened out again, stood an impressive mound covered with the debris of fallen masonry and low scrub growth. The men did not doubt that it once was a substantial dwelling, perhaps of many rooms and several stories, isolated at the highest spot on the mesa where occupation could possibly have occurred. The ruin was separated from the foot of Companion Rock by a twenty-foot-deep saddle in the sandstone surface of the mesa, above which soared the column. The collapsed structure promised productive exploration. Its siting on a barren rock platform hundreds of yards up from the nearest source of water was puzzling, but the view in all directions was breathtaking.

When Jeancon and Palmer returned, they called upon several ranchers working land on the Piedra terraces at the cuesta's western toe. One of these was a member of the Pargin family, who had come across the plains from Missouri after the Civil War and settled on the Piedra about 1902. He and his neighbors showed their visitors other sites that, although overgrown with sage, appeared to differ from those on the Chimney Rock mesa. A possible temporal distinction was implied. If verified, it would give archaeologists an opportunity to study a progression through time of regional culture.

Exhilarated by what he saw, Jeancon set about immediately to ready a field expedition. First, through the efforts of E. B. Renaud, professor of Romance languages, he secured the collaboration of the University of Denver. This institution aided in soliciting funds and provided five student field hands. One of these was Frank H. H. Roberts, Jr., later to become a stalwart in the formative period of Southwestern archaeology. Next, Jeancon worked through U.S. Senator L. C. Phipps of Colorado and Jesse Walter Fewkes, his former boss and head of the Bureau of American Ethnology at the Smithsonian Institution, to obtain an excavation permit from the U.S. Department of Agriculture. This agency had jurisdiction over the Chimney Rock environs because they were within a national forest. The Colorado highway department loaned the expedition a two-ton truck to haul necessary gear to the field and bring specimens back to Denver.

The Chimney Rock expedition was launched that June. In 1921 the roads away from the more settled areas along the east face of the Rockies were little more than wagon traces. The one over Wolf Creek Pass had been completed just five years earlier and was meant for automobiles. It was a dirt roadbed twelve feet wide with few places where vehicles going in opposite directions could pass. In some spots rocky outcrops projecting from the cliffs required soft car tops to be lowered. On the opposite side of the road were sheer drops of many hundreds of feet. The party needed two days to grind up the steep switchbacks. From Pagosa Springs on the south side to Chimney Rock, the road was worse. In wet weather it often took as many as fifty-two hours to go the twenty-two miles from town to the cuesta. That June was dry, however, and in a matter of half a day the excavators were on location. They pitched camp on a bench above Devil Creek at the northwest end of the mesa, where four men from the San Juan area, including Palmer, joined the ranks. The following three days were spent clearing an abandoned logging road so that all vehicles could reach the camp and building a mile-long footpath up the mesa to the archaeological sites on top.

Excavation began at the head of the trail with the opening of two circular-to-rectangular single-room structures, with some rough stone walls still standing up to seven feet in height. The rooms appeared to have served domestic functions because milling bins, stone grinding implements, fragments of pottery, a stone axe, one bone awl, and charred corn were found in them, along with hearths and a sandstone bench next to one wall. The floors were smoothed by a layer of adobe mud spread over the irregular caprock of the mesa. Each unit was roofed originally with an undetermined pattern of wooden poles covered with branches, earth, and sandstone slabs. Slab paving was noticed outside the rooms.

According to Jeancon's count, the vaguely round depressions indicating shelters on the mesa top numbered 107. Some were no more than ten feet in diameter; others were over forty feet across. Most had been placed along the east, west, and north edges of the prominence, the south part of the landform being unsuitable for architectural purposes because

The 1921 field camp of the State Historical and Natural History Society at the north base of the Chimney Rock pinnacles. *Courtesy University of Denver.*

of deep canyons slicing back into it. None of these stone-lined hollows was cleared of its overburden that season, though, because all hands were eager to get to work on the centerpiece mound high up in the shadow of the rocks.

A narrow ridge separating the lower and upper levels of the mesa top, with sheer slopes on either side and an incline projecting upward for seventy-five feet, struck Jeancon as a natural defense. He called it "the causeway." At its summit the party undertook to excavate the low walls of block masonry remaining from a circular room set within an oblong terrace. The room was elaborated with a small antechamber, a firepit, and a depressed pot rest. To judge from a modest assortment of artifacts taken from its fill, the usage was secular. Nevertheless, because of its strategic position blocking access to the upper mesa, on which the principal structure sat, Jeancon referred to the ruin as "the guardhouse."

The large pueblo on the uppermost, triangular mesa level proved to be a well-built, compact, L-shaped unit over two hundred feet long on its southern side. It was divided into an estimated thirty-five ground-level rooms, some commodious, others small. These wrapped around two circular ceremonial rooms, or kivas. The amount and type of debris in places confirmed a partial second story along the north side that had fallen. Some of the walls, of an estimated twenty on the upper level, were still standing up to fourteen feet in height. Their profiles were plumb, and their corners were squared but not bonded. They were constructed with an outer veneer surface of coursed thick and thin sandstone blocks broken from the matrix rock upon which the building was placed, over an inner core of stones and mud. Originally, wall surfaces were probably mud plastered; because of exposure and moisture, all such fragile coating was gone. Jeancon determined through careful inspection of all junctures that an exterior shell of the structure was put in place first, interior partitions being added subsequently. This studied approach implied a master plan, not a haphazard adding-on as the need arose. Since the pueblo stood on bare rock, floors had to be leveled by filling in uneven surfaces with mud. The entire floor then was thickly frosted with liquid adobe that hardened. A sufficient number of roof elements was found to hypothesize about its design: a pattern of primary and secondary beams topped with brush and a copious earthen layer.

Work of the 1921 season completely or partially cleared five of what were regarded primarily as dwellings, all notable for their large size (more than twenty feet in length). Two of these rooms produced such a noteworthy find of manos (grinding stones), metates (larger grinding slabs), and potsherds that they were believed to have been storage facilities. Additionally, ten small rectangular units surrounding the eastern kiva were emptied. These may have been used for storage; more likely they were filled with dirt and some crossbars to serve as reinforcing cellular buttresses to counter the outward thrust of the large kiva. They probably were roofed at the same level as the adjacent kiva to create a broad public space in front of the two-story roomblock to the north. Other work areas were at a premium because of the constriction of the mesa.

The eastern kiva was set down within a rectangular enclosure whose wall height matched that of the kiva. Given the placement of the village on bedrock, the kiva could not be sunk into the ground, and so the

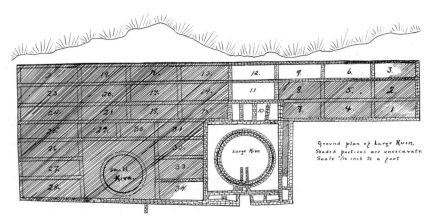

Jeancon's 1921 drawing of the ground plan of the Chimney Rock pueblo showing excavated rooms. *After Jeancon, 1922, Plate XII.*

subterranean effect had to be simulated by this means. Jeancon marveled that, without engineering equipment, the builders had erected a true circle. Walls were of fine coursed masonry, in one area still coated with mud plaster. A low bench encircled the base of the chamber, with horizontal beam rests spaced on top of it. Diggers encountered two floor levels resulting from remodeling. A pair of short horizontal tunnels, superimposed one above the other, projected into the chamber and connected at the other end into a single vertical shaft in the south wall. These provided necessary ventilation — there were no other openings to the chamber except a probable hatchway in the roof. The crew did not find a ceremonial floor opening to the spirit world, or *sipapu*, in either floor. They did find a hearth, but because it was not directly in line with the ventilator tunnel mouth, the vertical stone slab normally placed to prevent currents from blowing ash or smoke into the room was absent.

As for roof construction, the evidence suggested that four spaced upright posts had supported a square central frame, to which were attached horizontal beams penetrating the kiva walls, stabilized by short uprights secured in the bench-top beam rests. Over this basic roof skeleton lay a herringbone arrangement of small secondary timbers

Unusual trilobed abalone shell pendant or gorget recovered in the upper ventilator shaft of the east kiva of the Chimney Rock pueblo. The material must have been imported along lengthy trade channels from the Pacific Coast, but manufacture could have taken place anywhere en route, if not locally. *Courtesy Colorado Historical Society.*

covered with brush, earth, and an outer paving of unmortared sandstone slabs.

At the end of the season's exploration, Jeancon was convinced that the Chimney Rock pueblo, although distinct from its immediate neighbors, represented a local effort. He regarded the workmanship as excellent, the effort required to quarry stone in situ and to transport earth and water to the locale as staggering. Notwithstanding what he called "indigenous accomplishments," he also suspected an undefined relationship in the style of the Chimney Rock pueblo with that of Pueblo Bonito, the largest settlement in Chaco Canyon some ninety miles to the south (then being studied by a team sponsored by the National Geographic Society) and with that at Aztec Ruins, about forty miles to the southwest, where excavations had just halted.

Between the Chimney Rock pueblo and the place where the sandstone crust of the mesa drops sharply before rising into the bedding of

Companion Rock, the State Historical and Natural History Society crew observed a sizable depression where at one time raging fires had permanently reddened the stone. What happened there? Was rubbish burned? Unlikely. Both ancient and modern Pueblo Indians typically disposed of trash over the nearest cliff, in a heap in a nearby designated spot, in abandoned house rooms, or all around the outskirts. Were the fires ceremonial? Perhaps. The siting of the village in such difficult, awesome surroundings suggests a ritualistic intent. Did the Twin War Gods look down upon special rites? Was cremation of the dead one of them? Were the dead prisoners or protectors? Just below the adjacent northern rimrock, the field party discovered a two-hundred-foot-long strip of the sloughing mesa sides where a solidified mass of calcined human bones, pottery fragments, and other artifacts had accumulated. The diggers thought they detected clearings for pyres there. However, it is possible that the actual incineration of bodies took place somewhere else. Above, in the pit in naked rock? The improbable setting of the pueblo likewise could have been chosen with an eye to defense. If so, maybe the fires ignited on the Chimney Rock promontory served as signals to a network of allies? The plot to this story of the ancients of Chimney Rock decidedly thickened.

Down at the west base of the cuesta, preliminary observations confirmed the ranchers' reports of ruins, but the institution's team was astounded at their number. The men reconnoitered the first and second terraces south along both sides of the Piedra River, counting them by the dozens. However, compared to the Chimney Rock pueblo, these sites did not amount to much. They stood out as either small, low hillocks or circular pits blanketed with sage, generally the first plant to revegetate disturbed ground in the Southwest. Jagged chunks of burned adobe, some with beam impressions, and a few potsherds covered the surfaces. Some sites were strung out in a line along the bench tops. Others were clustered close together, on occasion rimming a depression of considerable circumference. Jeancon theorized that this particular settlement pattern represented single-family dwellings surrounding some sort of communal gathering place.

As they turned to the riverine remains, the student diggers found the going tougher and less exciting than at the Chimney Rock pueblo.

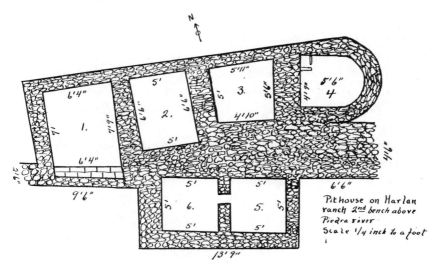

Jeancon's 1921 drawing of the ground plan of the Harlan ranch site at the western base of the Chimney Rock cuesta. *After Jeancon, 1922, Plate VI.*

The difficulty was due to the amorphous, ill-defined nature of the structures involved. Walls often were hard to trace, and shapes of rooms were unpredictable. The students found some one-room dwellings sunk a foot or more into the soil, with upper walls of rounded river cobbles slumped into great piles of mud and rock. Although Jeancon termed these structures "pithouses," later research elsewhere in the San Juan Basin restricted that definition to shelters of much greater depth wherein the surrounding earth formed walls and provided insulation. One mound covered what had been a complex of very small contiguous surface rooms made of variable combinations of adobe, cobblestone, and horizontally laid sandstone slabs. In some instances the walls still bore coats of mud plaster. The lack of connecting doorways suggested entrance through flat roofs made of poles, brush, and earth. Some floors were paved with pieces of sandstone glued into place with adobe mud, which, as any Southwesterner knows, is the stickiest of substances.

One unusual structure excavated in this first season was an isolated circular building approximately fifteen feet in diameter having very thick cobblestone walls that originally rose to an estimated height of ten feet. An interior hearth and an assortment of artifacts pointed to domestic occupation. Even so, Jeancon called this unit a tower, implying that he thought it something other than an ordinary family residence. To him, it was part of a defense system that probably incorporated many other comparable structures in the vicinity. By the end of the next season, he had decided that the sixty-five to seventy-five round structures of the mesa were indeed military towers. Towers also had been identified in the Mesa Verde province to the west of Chimney Rock and south on the Jemez Plateau of New Mexico. Whether they were erected to serve as lookout posts had not been determined.

Restricted digging in 1921 convinced Jeancon that further research would reveal at least six stages in the local prehistoric architectural development. His theorized chronology began with one-room dwellings partially set down into the ground and advanced to the above-ground multiroomed complex of carefully crafted sandstone masonry blocks. According to information at the time, Basketmaker culture was not represented in the former, but classic Pueblo was in the latter. Perhaps Jeancon did have evidence to fill the gap in between. He had no idea how long such an evolutionary process might have taken, nor did he entertain the possibility of contemporaneity. In that early period of researching the area's prehistory, a simplistic progression from crude to complex architecture was assumed and thought to have encompassed three or four thousand years.

Further substantiation of a cultural developmental sequence from early to late came through recovered pottery. Fragments from the so-called pithouses were coarse; Jeancon believed they were punched from a wad of clay rather than created by a coiling method. These fragments primarily were tiny, gray, and rough-surfaced, and the vessels presumably were used for storage or for cooking over open fires. Many pieces were warped out of shape because of the potter's carelessness or lack of skill. A few were decorated with crudely executed black designs on an untreated gray surface. Later forms were what Jeancon called heart-shaped jars with round bodies closing in to very small mouths, dippers made from a small bowl attached to a troughed handle that in cross-section duplicated a gourd sliced in half, and wide-mouthed, bag-shaped jars.

Unfired balls of clay, shaped by being thrust while moist into orifices of earthenware containers, also were recovered.

The pottery from the commanding pueblo beneath the stone columns was of better quality and, Jeancon believed, of a later time. Vessel size had increased. The number of shapes had expanded to include bladder-shaped jars, handled pitchers, and bowls. Utility types from that site retained the bag-shaped, tapered-bottom forms, but some had purposefully textured exteriors, with construction coils crimped successively as they were added upward in the pot's formation. However, a frequent diagonal patterning to the impressions made it appear as if the pots had been twisted in a screw. The interiors of these vessels were smoothed so as not to catch food particles. For some unknown reason, Jeancon referred to these as "flower pots." That was an unfortunate choice of words — the round-bottomed vessels could not have stood erect without yucca fiber rings or supporting depressions in earth, and there was no clue that the ancients raised flowers. He also unaccountably compared the pots to flat-bottomed, often highly decorated Chaco cylindrical vessels, which some modern students consider to be a specialized ceramic introduction from Mexico restricted to ceremonial use. Most Chimney Rock pueblo service vessels were enhanced with a set of simple black geometric patterns painted over a white slip that afforded greater contrast between ground and design and masked imperfections in the base material. Draftsmanship and format layout were improved over earlier pottery-making efforts. Again, Jeancon felt that some influence from the Chaco region was apparent in specific design motifs. He also was reminded of pottery from the Gallina area of northern New Mexico, where he had worked prior to his move to Colorado. Still, Jeancon asserted that Chimney Rock pottery remained distinctive enough to be recognizable. A fair number of fragments were red in color, and Jeancon at first considered these to have been parts of containers traded into the Chimney Rock district. Later he concluded that poorer specimens likely were native, an opinion subsequent theorists would reject.

Now and then the excavators exhumed human remains during the course of their investigations and took note of what they thought might be extensive burial reserves along the river benches. Some bones were so fragile that they crumbled upon being touched. Others were so well preserved that burial position and sex of the individual could be determined. Associated pottery offerings were occasionally collected. Jeancon interpreted the finds of calcined bone fragments, some strewn in beds of charcoal and ash, as evidence for the practice of cremation.

The State Historical and Natural History Society's work in the 1921 season aroused the curiosity of numerous people living in the Chimney Rock area, who long had felt their place had importance to other folks in other times. Jeancon said he showed more than five hundred of them through the digs. Considering the ruins' isolation and the difficulty of getting to them, he may have exaggerated that number to impress his board of directors.

On his return to Denver, Jeancon continued lobbying the board for what had become his pet project. Excitedly he reported to the members in a 1924 manuscript, "The Pagosa field is so far beyond the expectations, in extent, interest and accessibility, that your curator begs you to exert every means at your disposal to continue the work in that field. Here is the opportunity to do big things and Colorado has never had a bigger chance to place herself in the limelight as at this time." He assured the board that Alfred V. Kidder, then the most highly regarded scientist in the discipline, had stated that exploration of Archuleta County, incorporating the Chimney Rock–Piedra district, was the most important archaeological study then underway in the entire United States. This claim was also an overstatement, but it helped the board persuade the state legislature to appropriate $4,500 for another period of field work.

There were snags. A $700,000 shortfall was discovered in the state budget for 1922, and the researchers had to undertake a fund-raising drive. Enough public-spirited citizens responded with contributions that, with a complementary grant from the University of Denver, a total larger than that originally budgeted by the state was eventually amassed.

While the financing was in doubt, Jeancon fretted that someone else would usurp rights in what he then thought of as his personal research domain. Palmer, for one, had applied for an excavation permit to dig in the Chimney Rock area. Jeancon urgently contacted his friend Fewkes and was successful in getting the application denied on the grounds that Palmer was not academically trained or institutionally connected.

Meanwhile, the State Historical and Natural History Society was granted its own two-year permit, with the proviso that work commence within thirty days. With no money in hand, it seemed unlikely that the condition could be met. Jeancon protested to all who would listen that out-of-staters were robbing Colorado of its patrimony. It was a fact that much of the regional archaeology of the time was carried on by persons from Eastern institutions; up until the previous year Jeancon himself had been among them. Jeancon furthered his argument by noting that foreign governments were also benefiting from the state's antiquities, a reference to a collection of Mesa Verde artifacts sent to Sweden thirty years earlier. In the end, the necessary funds were collected, and at the beginning of the summer a field party returned to the camp below the feet of the stone columns.

The first order of business in 1922 was a brief reconnaissance of the upper San Juan drainage around Pagosa Junction to the southeast of Chimney Rock and along the Pine River to the west. In the first locality local diggers previously had unearthed samples of crude black-on-white pottery from pithouse depressions sprinkled over several acres. Along the Pine near the modern Ute agency at Ignacio, recent Anglo and Native American activity had disturbed older remains of what seemed to have been cobblestone or adobe structures and a scattering of discarded fragments of earthenware, grinding tools, and debitage. Although no excavations were done, the survey confirmed a widely distributed ancient culture in some respects similar to and probably contemporaneous with much of that at Chimney Rock.

At the focal location on the Piedra River, exploration was initiated at three groups of mounds on the first east terrace above the river. One group was on a spur of the foothills to the north of the Pagosa-Durango road. Two additional mound complexes were a couple miles south of the Harlan ranch, where work had been carried out the previous summer. Discoveries at two of these places elaborated on the earlier findings of adobe and cobblestone pithouses and sandstone-slab upper walls resting on cobble foundations. The third site consisted of surface rooms whose masonry of coursed thin and thick blocks was not unlike that of the Chimney Rock pueblo. In his report on this ruin, Roberts, who had returned for a second time, speculated that it was of a late stage in the

Black-on-white vessel in the shape of a mountain sheep with an upturned nose taken in 1922 from a burial at a site at the western base of the Chimney Rock mesa. A handle originally attached the head to the body. One ear is partly broken off. The wavy lines are thought to represent fur. A solid triangular element with a negative stepped central motif runs down the back. Specimen stands 8.25 inches in height and is 6.5 inches long. *Courtesy Colorado Historical Society.*

local sequence. This judgment was considered likely in future work, not just because of the advanced type of construction but also because ceramics retrieved from three burials were finer. These included a charming black-on-white hollow figurine of a mountain sheep, some black-on-white bowls with expertly drawn, more compact patterns, and jars of what were then called "coiled ware." Such pottery later was termed "corrugated" and determined to be an innovation of the Pueblo II stage of development (see Chapter 3). A tiny piece of turquoise taken from one burial further suggested to researchers at that time a temporal placement postdating the pithouse culture.

In all the terrace settlements dug to that date no structure that could be regarded as a kiva as defined elsewhere on the Colorado Plateau was

Partially excavated Chimney Rock pueblo, ca. 1922. East kiva is in foreground. Figure in background may be J. A. Jeancon. *Courtesy Colorado Historical Society.*

exposed. However, there was a frequently repeated pattern of circular depressions banked on at least two sides with low swales. Conceivably, these once might have been subterranean ceremonial chambers, each with its complement of surface user dwellings. The larger of these depressions were suggested to have been open-air plazas or courtyards where community dances took place. For the time being, definitive answers to these matters were put aside for future inquiry.

Back at the Chimney Rock pueblo on its lofty perch above the guardhouse, work continued in the row of cubicles between the two kivas and in the west kiva itself. Here some standing walls comprised eleven feet of coursed masonry, making excavation quite a different job from trying to trace the often elusive outlines of the shallow floors and crumbled cobblestone walls of the structures down in the valley. The walls in the west part of the Chimney Rock edifice were not as well

A large duck-shaped jar recovered in pieces in 1922 at the Chimney Rock pueblo further convinced Jeancon that this site was somehow related with those in Chaco Canyon. Because of the use of a vegetal pigment, later research suggests an origin somewhere in the neighboring northwestern San Juan area. *Courtesy Colorado Historical Society.*

constructed as those in the eastern portion, implying an earlier building episode. Large accumulations of refuse were deposited within them, suggesting that this series of chambers had become a communal dump for a considerable period of time before the final abandonment of the rest of the village. The western kiva lacked some of the features found in its eastern counterpart, but it did have a raised firebox and a southern ventilator shaft. The latter did not have an attached horizontal floor-level tunnel. Part of the kiva floor had been put over a bed of sand used to smooth the uneven caprock subsurface. Charred fallen timbers indicated a cribbed roof structure. Unfortunately, dendrochronology was an unproven means of dating in 1922, and bits of beams and other building timbers, as well as chunks of charcoal, were removed and tossed aside. Jeancon felt confident that he had found an outpost of Chaco culture, writing in 1924, "The result of the studies at Aztec and Chaco show that the Chimney Rock people were undoubtedly related to both of these areas. Similarity in pottery designs and forms, masonry, and house plans establish their relationship."

Within a few months after excavations ceased at the Chimney Rock pueblo, the old house began to deteriorate. The covering of fallen rocks and timbers and wind-deposited earth protecting it for centuries had been removed. Recognizing the problem, Jeancon advised the U.S. Forest Service to undertake immediate preservation measures. He observed that these would be time-consuming and expensive; water needed to mix cement mortar for re-laying walls would have to be hauled by burro more than a mile from the Piedra up the steep trail to the site. Recognition of these twentieth-century difficulties underscored the tremendous amount of effort that had been expended by the aboriginal builders, who lacked beasts of burden and canvas water bags or wooden kegs to help them get water to the heights.

As Jeancon pointed out, an alternative method for supplying water to the modern masons would be to build a road. With improved access, other ruins could be repaired more easily and the entire complex could be set aside as an archaeological preserve for public visitation. Baring an undercurrent of professional jealousy that has plagued the science since its inception, Jeancon wrote that he hoped it would be a state park rather than being added to the young national park system because he felt that Jesse L. Nusbaum, superintendent of Mesa Verde National Park, would adamantly oppose continuation of the Society's work. Jeancon need not have worried. The Chimney Rock pueblo was not repaired, a road was not built, and the Colorado legislature had no interest in proprietorship of a state park.

The next year, Jeancon sent out a survey headed by Frank Roberts that included Roberts's brother, Henry, and two friends. It was his first solo effort in the field, and quite surely he felt his oats. He was young and undaunted by the assignment Jeancon gave him: locating all prehistoric remains over varied terrain stretching 150 square miles from where the San Juan River gushed down out of the Rockies to its passage through the arid lands at the Utah border. A preliminary examination the previous season had produced promising results. Roberts equipped his little expedition with two Model T Ford touring cars and piled grub boxes, shovels, tents, and other paraphernalia in the back seats and on the running boards. He and his companions decked themselves out in the stereotypical exploration attire of the times — knee-high laced

Frank H. H. Roberts, Jr. *Smithsonian Institution photo 92–6038.*

boots, riding breeches, and felt campaign hats. This equipment was a step down from the pith helmets, swaths of mosquito netting, and phalanxes of colorful native workers characterizing the popular view of archaeologists being nurtured by Sunday newspaper photogravures of "lost cities" and King Tut's tomb (opened just a year earlier). Nevertheless, an air of romance attached itself to even such a humble venture in the U.S. West.

Departing from Pagosa Springs in mid-June 1923, the two-car convoy bounced over the dirt road going south along the western plateaus rimming the San Juan. Roberts wisely stopped at each of the cultivated patches belonging to the Archuletas, Aguirres, Gallegos, Quintanas, and other Hispanos to inquire whether in the course of digging ditches, installing fencing, or tending flocks of sheep the owners might have noticed Indian ruins or relics; if so, he and his colleagues would like permission to examine them. Everyone, it seemed, knew of something

Ducks share a 1923 Roberts farm camp. *Courtesy Colorado Historical Society.*

relevant and was eager to tell of it. Passing along from family to family, the Roberts party slowly made its way westward from the bend of the river at the hamlet of Trujillo, where the first ruins were observed. Sometimes the diggers camped overnight in the settlers' yards, where drinking water and shade were available.

At summer's end, Roberts and his team had placed hundreds of archaeological sites on their maps. Work concentrated on the tributaries as far west as the Animas, beyond which other investigators had made earlier reconnaissances. The remains recorded were of three types. One set of remains came from a relatively brief, limited intrusion of Navajos and Pueblos following the temporary expulsion of the Spaniards from the northern Rio Grande Valley at the end of the seventeenth century. The other two resulted from an extensive prehistoric occupation along the main course of the San Juan and its principal laterals. These sites appeared to correspond to that at the base of the Chimney Rock cuesta. Older and more numerous, these remains were characteristic of what was then being called the Pre-Pueblo horizon: low, heavily eroded mounds that Roberts thought resulted from decay of pithouses. Some were found in the floodplains, where they had been churned up by modern plowing. More often they were isolated on successive terraces retreating back from the watercourses. Many of these were at a considerable distance from the water. Beneath the sage covering these mounds, the surveyors noticed many clods of burned adobe and scattered fragments of pottery and broken stone tools. Without digging, Roberts decided that the dwellings mantled by the accumulation of burned soil had been constructed with the jacal method, in which spaced vertical posts are sealed into thick layers of mud. Conspicuous depressions of up to sixty feet across were either in the center or to one side of the mound clusters. Less frequent were disintegrated surface buildings made of courses of sandstone slabs or cobbles held together with masses of adobe mud.

Two observations were particularly intriguing because they paralleled similar features on the Chimney Rock mesa. On a point of Montezuma Mesa, rising abruptly from the riverbed of the San Juan and allowing a vast horizon-to-horizon vista, Roberts happened onto a spot in the rocky surface where huge conflagrations once had occurred. At a short distance was a ruin mound. He could not but wonder if the burn area had been a signaling station for the neighboring village and if it might have been part of a communications network reaching as far north as Chimney Rock. Flames or smoke could not have been seen directly between these two locales, but perhaps in the unexplored intervening wilderness there was another station. The other feature of special interest matching one on the Chimney Rock mesa top was a small circular cup very obviously cut into bedrock of Haystack Mountain near the town of Allison. Both bowls were about half a foot deep. In neither instance were there signs that the holes had been used as grinding mortars. Whatever other purpose they might have served remained a mystery.

More recent vestiges of the past were the sixteenth-century or early-seventeenth-century forked-stick hogans attributed to the Navajos and the rectangular coursed-masonry rooms perched on top of impregnable heights believed to have been erected by Rio Grande Pueblo peoples hiding from Spanish overlords. Sherds picked up in some of these places suggested that Jemez Pueblo residents had lived in them. Petroglyphs carved into cliff faces were identifiable as the work of Navajos, who prior to the Roberts survey were not known ever to have moved north of the San Juan River. The archaeological team also found clues to a period of European influence — settlers showed them yucca fiber ropes braided in typical Spanish fashion and a beaten copper plate.

The greatest concentration of ruins was found in the Piedra River valley. From the confluence of this stream with the San Juan, where the community of Arboles grew over a group of pithouses, north to where the valley pinched down at Chimney Rock, an unbroken line of pithouse mounds and heaps of stone houses stood on east and west benches. Also observed were several examples of Navajo or Pueblo occupation and rock art dating to the late seventeenth century, as well as probable nineteenth-century Ute camps. The men saw a masonry complex with standing six-foot-high walls on a high ledge to the west of the river opposite Chimney Rock and another on the crest of Coal Hill to its south. Both sites were reminiscent of and probably coeval with the houseblock up by the pinnacles. Thirty mounds spread over the flat plateau of Stollsteimer Mesa southwest of the Chimney Rock cuesta hinted at rather sizable Pre-Pueblo villages and seemed to Roberts to be potentially important in rounding out the prehistory of the district.

The next summer Roberts again spent three weeks doing some superficial digging on Stollsteimer Mesa but was called upon to finish the areal survey before much was accomplished. Four years passed before he returned to the Piedra area.

Meanwhile, Jeancon was back on Devil Creek in 1925 after a disappointing fund drive. He was discouraged with a legislature that annually promised and then withdrew research allotments and a lack of public appreciation for regional archaeology. In spite of the mounting

Unexcavated ruin mound on Stollsteimer Mesa, ca. 1924. At right rear, an abandoned pole-and-mud structure originally may have been erected by an early-day Hispanic settler. *Courtesy Colorado Historical Society.*

evidence for important aboriginal habitation in the upper San Juan region, no sites had been found with the glamorous appeal of the Mesa Verde cliff dwellings or the tumbled-down apartment houses baking in the sun of Chaco Canyon. Such sites might have spurred substantial financial contributions. The Chimney Rock pueblo was the sole contender for headlines, but it yielded few of the material things that curators and interested laymen equated with significance. Data was merely for the ivory-tower types — or so Jeancon concluded as he pondered resigning his position at the State Historical and Natural History Society.

In 1925 Jeancon and a crew of local workers trenched one of the round depressions frequently found near house mounds. When cleared, the sunken space was some six feet deep and twenty feet in diameter. Large river cobbles ringed the depression, which was paved with stones covered with a thick layer of hard-packed adobe. A fire hearth was centered on this floor. From the lower level a five-foot-wide terrace sloped up to an encircling bank, or bench, which in turn graded up to ground level. Jeancon's typescript of the excavation does not mention any evidence for a superstructure of walls and roof. Rectangular one-roomed dwellings with slightly sunken floors and post-and-mud walls were immediately adjacent. Jeancon interpreted the site as a pithouse village with a dance courtyard, which he called the "Plaza Grande." His informal paper notes, "The whole mesa top, on which Plaza Grande is situated, is almost a solid mass of ruins, mostly of the fourth period. Associated with Plaza Grande proper are two, or possibly three, more

View toward the west showing the 1925 clearing of the site containing Jeancon's "Plaza Grande" on a tongue of the Chimney Rock cuesta, with Petersen Mesa rising beyond the Piedra River. *Courtesy Colorado Historical Society.*

circular areas which appear to be the same sort of thing. No excavating was done in these places. There are also many detached single and double houses as well as several fairly large groups, one of which was excavated in 1921."

On the second terrace above the Harlan ranch, the party explored a second so-called tower. It possessed the same dimensions, cobblestone walls, and interior embellishments as the structure dug out in 1921. Instead of being isolated, as was the first construction, this one was associated with small cobblestone and adobe rooms and placed in a strategic spot controlling access to some trails up the Chimney Rock cuesta. The pottery recovered was primarily utilitarian ware. Jeancon described it as being bullet-shaped, with coils laid up in a wavy indented manner and furrowed perpendicularly by the potter's fingers. Future researchers named this ceramic type "Payan Corrugated" and found it typical of the late archaeological phases of the upper San Juan Basin.

In 1927 the Pecos Conference, a gathering of forty-five individuals then engaged in research dealing with some aspect of the prehistoric Southwest, worked out a standardized terminology and developmental sequence that helped place the Piedra district antiquities in their proper relationship to others scattered across the Colorado Plateau. Roberts, who attended that conference, had just excavated a pithouse village at the eastern end of Chaco Canyon, which he confidently placed in the newly defined Basketmaker III stage. He believed that with further exploration on Stollsteimer Mesa, he could bring the cultural record forward in time to the next stage, formerly called Pre-Pueblo but now

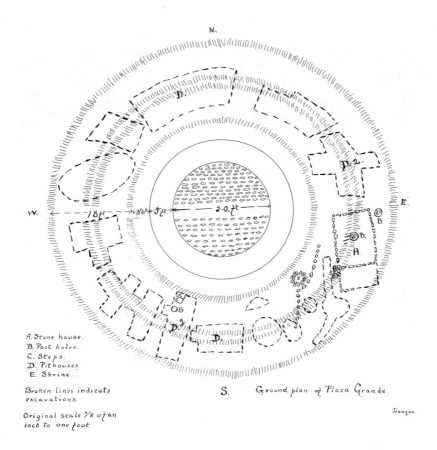

N.

A. Stone house.
B. Post holes.
C. Steps.
D. Pithouses.
E. Shrine.

Broken lines indicate
excavations.

Original scale 1/8 of an
inch to one foot

S.   Ground plan of Plaza Grande.

Jeançon.

N.   S.

a. Imaginary line over top of mounds.   *Jeançon*
b. Top of fill in dance plaza.
c. mounds over house remains.
d. Original earth.
e. Cobble paving.   Cross Section of Plaza Grande.

Fig. 2.

Previously unpublished Jeancon drawing of his 1925 excavations at the lower Chimney Rock cuesta site containing what was then described as a dance plaza. *Courtesy Colorado Historical Society.*

Cleared basal walls of cobbles and mud of what Jeancon in 1925 interpreted as a tower structure. In center foreground are several milling bins containing metates and manos. The Chimney Rock pinnacles are visible at left rear. *Courtesy Colorado Historical Society.*

designated as Pueblo I. Therefore, the digging season of 1928 saw him back where his archaeological career began.

During the four-year interval between visits to Stollsteimer Mesa, Roberts had spent two seasons in Chaco Canyon for the National Geographic Society expedition, finished a doctorate in anthropology at Harvard University, and taken a job at the Smithsonian's Bureau of American Ethnology in Washington. Jeancon carried out his threat to resign from the State Historical and Natural History Society, by then renamed the Colorado Historical Society, and his successor, Paul Martin, moved field operations to the Four Corners. With government money available and other professional claims on the territory eliminated, Roberts secured permission to work on the Southern Ute Indian Reservation, of which Stollsteimer Mesa was a part. He hired a local Hispanic crew and plunged into a prodigious excavation program. By the end of the summer eighty dwellings, two kivas, six circular depressions, and seven cemeteries had been explored.

Three related but distinct architectural types were present in the villages. Roberts considered them sequential: two were of the Pueblo I horizon, and one evolved into early Pueblo II. Entire communities into which these house types were clustered had burned either during occupancy, upon abandonment, or in the ensuing centuries. In some cases, it appeared to Roberts that the residents had been caught by the flames just after a fall harvest. Pots filled with corn kernels, beans, and various seeds lined the walls. Because the devastation was so complete, he felt it was evidence of warfare. The fires so hardened the earth partially or

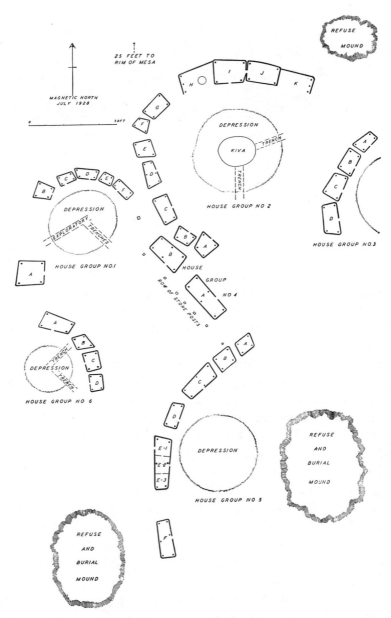

Drawing of Pueblo I village on Stollsteimer Mesa. *After Roberts,*
1930, Plate 3.

36

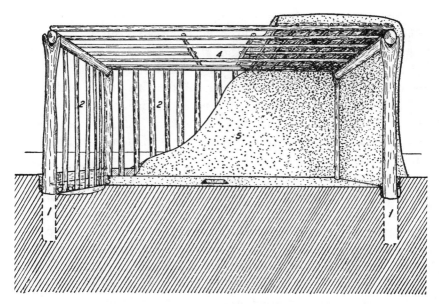

Roberts's reconstruction of an early Pueblo II jacal house type on Stollsteimer Mesa. In sequence, his numbers indicate main support posts, small wall poles, roof timbers, opening for smoke hole, and mud-plastered wall. *After Roberts, 1930, Figure 6.*

totally encasing wooden frameworks that beam impressions were retained, providing an accurate picture of construction. One-room quadrangular to rectangular detached surface units were the rule. Walls were of jacal, with some lateral door openings in them. The doors themselves were large stone slabs. Roofs were flat, made of posts and brush covered with earth, and pierced with a central smoke hole directly over a fire hearth on the floor. In the two earliest types, floors were cupped a foot or so into the surrounding surface. Some exceptionally small rooms with no ground-level door or hearth were probably storage chambers. In the most recent dwelling style, the storage rooms were made of unshaped rocks set in large amounts of adobe. Roberts saw these structures as the first local attempts at masonry.

The typical settlement pattern was a crescent around or near a yawning depression that, Roberts suggested, resulted from digging and puddling the huge amounts of earth needed for this kind of construction.

He came to the conclusion that most of these pits became reservoirs trapping runoff from rains and snowmelt. Because the villages were a considerable distance above either the Piedra River or Stollsteimer Creek and because no aboriginal trash was dumped into the pits, the reservoir hypothesis seemed plausible. Roberts found no evidence to support Jeancon's idea that the depressions were dance plazas. Trenching revealed only two instances where the Indians had converted the pits into what may have been early versions of a kiva. More likely, they were pithouses.

As usual in sites situated in the open, pottery was the most abundant type of recovered artifact. Having just completed a masterful analysis of Chaco ceramics for his dissertation, Roberts devoted a second study to those of Stollsteimer Mesa. He found that architecture and pottery together delineated the Pueblo I and early Pueblo II periods there. Many of the characteristics the Pecos Conference listed as diagnostic for those periods were obvious in this sherd lot: coils in neck areas of utility jars, rather than being obliterated, were retained for decorative effect and reinforcement; white slip was used to mask gray body ground; vessel shapes were more varied and larger; painted designs were timid and poorly drawn in early phases but grew bolder and more elaborate through time; and corrugated exteriors of cooking and storage receptacles were introduced.

The benches beside the Piedra held not only the physical remains of numerous prehistoric settlements but also the bones of their occupants. In layered fashion, that testimony of life and death carries through to modern times: the Hispanic village of Stollsteimer impinges on a Pueblo I dwelling group, and the Catholic chapel and its cemetery cover a midden used as its burying ground.

Elsewhere, the crew unearthed more than one hundred human skeletons in refuse mounds within each village precinct. For religious reasons the ancient Piedra dead were buried within trash deposits, composed of daily discards. Death was regarded as a continuation of the human cycle, and it was not considered disrespectful to inter them with the physical goods of earthly life. Furthermore, the trash deposits afforded easier digging with a stick than hard, compacted ground. Generally bodies were buried in flexed positions and sometimes accompanied

Pottery vessels recovered from Pueblo I–early Pueblo II sites on Stollsteimer Mesa: a) undecorated seed jar with eleven holes around orifice, possibly for insertion of feathers; b) bag-shaped utility jar with corrugated base and unindented coiled upper body; c) white-slipped small bowl bearing encircling black decoration executed in mineral pigment. *Courtesy Colorado Historical Society.*

Pottery vessels recovered from Pueblo I–early Pueblo II sites on Stollsteimer Mesa: a) black-on-white canteen; b) black-on-white pitcher; c) corrugated seed jar; d) undecorated dipper; e) plain utility jar. *Courtesy University of Denver.*

with simple offerings. Most skulls had been artificially flattened in infancy to produce the broad-headed Puebloan profile. At that time the few not so treated were considered a resilient Basketmaker strain.

Occasionally graves yielded mystifying or intriguing results that made excavators yearn to reach across silenced generations. One was a small pit into which had been wedged two male skulls and four earthenware vessels. What could possibly have been the tragic story behind this burial? Were the men victims of crime, accident, or warfare? Were they killed during a hunt far away from home, making transport of their entire bodies too burdensome? Another burial of special interest was that of a man who obviously had been a person of consequence in the community. He was interred with a cache of well-made projectile points, bone-knapping tools, twenty-one pieces of pottery, red ochre, and the bones of a golden eagle.

Years and the elements of nature had distilled the transitory presence of hundreds of individuals in the Piedra district into a pitiful few stumps of walls, bits and pieces of imperishable objects used to get from day to day, withered foodstuffs that even rodents or weevils had ignored, and the terminal contribution of human bones. Even with such an incomplete assemblage of evidence, at the end of what was to be his last field endeavor in the region, Roberts felt his work had illuminated a few pages of the earliest chapter of Pueblo life. It was a confused time when change from the Basketmaker mode to something more elaborate was taking place. The surveys and digs substantiated a shift from the deep pithouses used elsewhere to slightly depressed to above-ground chambers, from jacal to masonry architecture, from detached to contiguous rooms in linear plans. Additionally, a cultural advancement similar to that others were exposing on many adjacent arteries of the San Juan was identified. It was generally agreed that at some period in the past, people pursuing a lifeway categorized as Pueblo I spread throughout this fertile but demanding part of Colorado. The Piedrans had neighbors in other drainages. Perhaps jacal architecture remained in vogue longer in northeastern sectors because of plentiful timber supplies and a scarcity of easily fractured stone. Perhaps some small handicrafts, such as pottery, did not evolve as rapidly there as in other parts of the northern Southwest because geographical isolation and small-scale occupation denied artisans the stimuli of crossroads centers. Still, it seemed to Roberts and his contemporaries that across the Colorado Plateau the ancients somehow had marched through time in relative cultural unison. It would not be until the year after research on the Piedra ceased that dendrochronology began to supply calendar dates that set the record straight.

3

ANASAZI UNDER WATER

Water is an enemy of antiquities. Yet, paradoxically, the threat of impounded water proved to be a boon to the unraveling of the prehistory of the upper San Juan district.

In 1956 Congress enacted legislation to construct the Navajo Dam on the San Juan River as part of the Upper Colorado River Storage Project. A lake some thirty-four miles long was expected to back up behind that construction to the 6,100-foot elevation contour, flooding the lower Pine River canyon and spreading approximately six miles north and east of the merger of the Piedra with the main stem of the San Juan. Ten lesser side channels also were to be inundated. The dam's inlets, outlets, spillways, diversion tunnel, and coffer dam would further disturb the natural topography. By the 1950s the environmental movement had gained sufficient strength to demand the recordation or recovery of whatever archaeological or historical resources might be submerged before they were sacrificed forever on the altar of modern irrigation and recreation needs. Because the area to be most affected lay in New Mexico, the Department of the Interior contracted with the School of American Research and then the Museum of New Mexico, both in Santa Fe, to do the job. Dr. A. E. Dittert, Jr., served as director.

The location of the San Juan uplands on the border of the Anasazi world and the absence there of large structures, other than the unique Chimney Rock pueblo beyond the reach of the Navajo Reservoir, had doomed them to virtual archaeological oblivion following the pioneering work of Frank Roberts. But multiyear government funding provided the impetus for scientific examination of a previously ignored region, where a human presence was suspected to have been in place for many

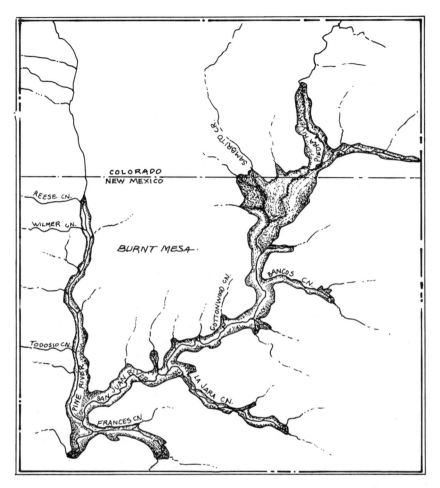

Map of Navajo Reservoir on San Juan River and tributaries in relation to Chimney Rock Archeological Area. *Courtesy U.S. Forest Service.*

centuries prior to the arrival of white dam builders. From 1957 through 1962 teams of archaeologists and support personnel took to this field, with another three years devoted to laboratory analysis and reporting. The results helped explain the background of the Chimney Rock prehistory.

Archaeological reconnaissance in rough terrain lacking an adequate road network was not without its problems. Getting from here to there

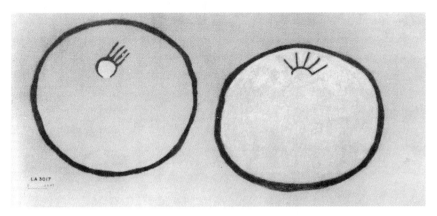

The concept of the Twin War Gods, depicted in a now-submerged pictograph on a cliff beside the San Juan River (Site LA 3017), was borrowed by modern Navajos from the Pueblo Indian cosmology that possibly was rooted in the Anasazi past. *After Schaafsma 1963, Figure 36.*

often meant slogging step by step. Surveyors were transported to a drainage mouth and picked up hours or days later at its head. In summer heat they plodded up and down embankments, forded and reforded rocky streams with boots dripping wet and feet threatened with fungus, tramped broad sagebrush flats, and laboriously scrambled to lofty mesa tops as they meticulously scanned the ground for bits of telltale evidence of former occupation. The lower canyon of the Pine was particularly troublesome because its narrow, sheer-walled gut defied access. The resourceful men then converted the museum field jeep into an amphibious craft by attaching a vertical extension to its exhaust pipe; it might get hung up on a rock, but with luck it would not drown. One can only wonder at what the astounded aborigines would have thought of that noisy monster charging upriver past their stumpy hillocks of corn struggling to grow on the narrow benches above the water.

Work commenced near the dam site because extensive borrow operations in the bed and terraces of the river would be needed to get material for what was then to be the second-largest earth-fill dam ever built by the Bureau of Reclamation. In the first season thirteen prehistoric sites were excavated and forty-seven others were noted as ravenous equipment sat ready to move in and devour them. Eventually, nearly seven hundred places where ancient people had hunted, lived, worked, or died were plotted on a field map, twenty-one of which were either cleared or tested. Artifacts discarded from this parade of life were processed. A huge file of photographs was compiled. Panels of rock art pecked into or painted on cliff faces were recorded, among them Navajo depictions of the Twin War Gods. Evidence for perhaps five or more millennia of man's habitation of the upper San Juan corner of the Colorado Plateau had been obtained.

PALEO-INDIAN, ARCHAIC PERIODS
CA. 3000 B.C.-A.D. 1

The Museum of New Mexico party did not find Paleo-Indian lithic remains within the Navajo Reservoir pool confines, but they have since been recovered in small quantities in nearby areas. Evidence from adjacent parts of the San Juan Basin suggests that ancient hunters wandered there in search of large game, primarily bison, for some thousands of years before the Christian Era. Eventually environmental changes led to a decrease in the size of the bison herds, causing the nomads either to drift eastward toward the grassy Great Plains or modify their basic food-gathering patterns in order to sustain themselves otherwise. In the case of the latter adjustment, they slowly developed a way of life typifying the Archaic period.

In the Navajo Reservoir district the Archaic was characterized by a few thin deposits of hearth litter (rock that had been splintered by fire), earth discolored by disintegrating charcoal, fragments of projectile points, and a scattering of pecked and ground stone implements. The limited number of Archaic use zones, restricted to mesa crests in the southern sectors of the dam project, suggested intermittent wandering bands of people with a low-level technology for gaining and preparing the wherewithal for daily survival. The projectile points spoke of a diet of small fauna, and the milling stones would be used to grind leaves, stems, berries, and wild nuts. Finds in other regional Archaic sites indicate that maize corn may have been grown there as early as 1000

B.C. but probably in a restricted way that did not interfere with the more important seasonal foraging. The San Juan drainage cut through upland and lowland terrain suitable for a combination of the two fundamental life support systems, horticulture and hunting-gathering. However, as the cultivation of corn assumed greater significance because of its predictability, the need to stay full-time in one place increased, and seminomadic Archaic bands metamorphosed into the sedentary Anasazi.

Los PINOS PHASE (BASKETMAKER II) CA. A.D. 150–400

At about the same time the Romans were tossing Christians to the lions on the other side of the world, some players emerged from behind the scenes of the earlier shadowy Paleo-Indian and Archaic periods to commence a thousand-year run on the San Juan stage. By the time Rome was sacked, these men and women already were firmly committed to a revolutionary shift away from rootless nomadism to a lifestyle increasingly anchored by simple horticulture and sedentism. Somewhere else, maybe along the foothills of the San Juan Mountains, they had learned how to plant kernels of corn and squash seeds to produce important supplements to whatever undomesticated edibles were available. With growing seasons of up to 150 days in length and a perennial water supply, the floodplains and terraces beside the San Juan corridors offered a favorable microenvironment. Somewhere else, these people cleverly had learned to create shelters for themselves out of the earth, rocks, and timbers around them. This, too, may have been part of a cultural growth that took place a short distance away.

Researchers working with these particular San Juan remains referred to them as examples of the Los Pinos Phase, or Basketmaker II as defined in the Pecos Classification. At first, the lower Pine River region seemed the center of this occupation, but later investigation put the heartland further north, near the small modern community of Bayfield and closer to a second comparable development in the environs of Durango. The term "phase" implied that it was one step in a long cultural evolution by a single physical stock. After the mid-1930s the entire prehistoric continuum on the Colorado Plateau was called "Anasazi" rather than being split into Basketmaker and Pueblo categories. Regardless of the stage taxonomy devised to artificially order data, there was no sharply defined delineation between one period of development and the next but rather a subtle growth process.

The earliest of the regional prehistoric dwellings, recorded at twenty-three sites, were situated on the edges of benches above the floodplains through which the few watercourses flow. The novice farmers of the era presumably prepared and tended garden parcels down below, where there was arable land and little arboreal vegetation. In those locations the plants benefited from runoff trickling down the cliffs, seasonal flooding of the river, and high water tables near the streams. The randomly scattered one-room houses were either vaguely circular, circular with a small rounded antechamber separated from the main room by a hallway demarked by rows of upright poles, or figure-eight in shape. Their earthen floors were slightly scooped below ground level. Exterior dwelling walls were made of dry-laid cobbles leaned against a cribbed wood framework or of river cobbles held in vertical position by wads of adobe mud over a foundation of logs placed in a channel gouged into the ground. Bands of stones ringing a few structures were first thought to have been a purposefully installed paving, but most likely they represented fallen walls. The builders created some interior partitions with closely spaced upright wooden timbers, stuffing the interstices with worn basket fragments and corn cobs, which then were encased with mud. Because the diameter of the units averaged some twenty-seven feet, roofing them demonstrated an impressive degree of practical engineering skill. The feat probably was accomplished with horizontally laid cribbed logs secured in position by nothing more than placement and weight to form a dome or truncated superstructure with a central smoke hole/entryway. Occasional indications of trouble loomed overhead, where irregularly placed holes in the dirt floor indicate, it is believed, where emergency vertical roof braces may have been installed.

Pits of various forms pockmarked the floors. Some were smoothed with mud that hardened, others were rimmed with sandstone slabs, and

Los Pinos Phase (Basketmaker II) Albino Village pithouse (Site LA 4269), upper Pine River section of the Navajo Reservoir district, with encircling ring of cobbles. *Courtesy Museum of New Mexico.*

still others were untreated. Several above-ground cupboards were fashioned from concentric coils of mud, gradually tapering in circumference to make a beehive form. Fire-reddened walls suggested that excavated pits with a restricted mouth and undercut sides may have been the Crockpots of the day. Sandstone slabs or clay plugs sealed various cists from rodents, who would recklessly have gambled on escaping the cooking pits. These humble pits, and others found outside the houses, reveal two important qualities of this period. First, gathering and/or

Schematic drawing of cut-away and roofed pithouse. *Courtesy U.S. Forest Service.*

farming yielded surpluses needing to be held over from one season to the next either as seed stock or as foodstuffs. Second, thought was given not only to living today but continuing to exist tomorrow. The ability to look to a future, however clouded, was a clue to the cultural progress of the first more-or-less settled inhabitants of the upper San Juan.

Crude as the dwellings were, they were a major advancement over open-air camps. They afforded protection and must have been reasonably comfortable cocoons in winter, with fire basins, body heat, only one exterior opening, and the insulating properties of earth and stone. However, open hearths and exposed wooden roofing elements turned them into fire traps. Some seasonality in their use is possible, and the term of tenure may have been brief. Nevertheless, the considerable energy invested in the erection of the domiciles points to their having been regarded as permanent.

The bulk of portable manufactured objects from the Los Pinos Phase ruins were of stone. They exhibited able craftsmanship in their formation and performed a wide range of functions. Spear points, blades, and choppers were used for hunting, skinning out the bag, and butchering it for consumption. Game animals probably were dispatched by an atlatl and spear. Deer, with their taste for the plentiful scrubby browse of the mesa tops (now locally called buck bush), were the most likely targets. Scrapers and knives were made for working hides, and grinding slabs and hand stones for pulverizing corn and wild seeds. Their proportionately high number reflects the importance of gathering and small-scale horticulture. Hammers, abraders, and cores were the tools needed to form other stone implements; drills, scrapers, and choppers cut and shaped wooden objects; and round cobbles helped smooth and compact construction mud. Sharp-pointed bone awls served in the preparation of articles of animal hides and in the weaving of baskets. Baskets themselves were not recovered intact because exposure in open settings obliterated the remains, but a number of impressions of them were observed on hardened clods of adobe mud applied as part of the jacal construction.

Pottery was absent from the artifact assemblage at these sites except in late horizons, when a few pieces of brown wares apparently began to be produced. They were among the earliest earthenware made in the northern Southwest.

A few collapsed walls, several hundred stone artifacts, and impressions of corn cobs in fire-hardened adobe or corn pollen found near several burials constitute a paltry index to several hundred years or more of human activity. By drawing analogies with modern peoples, one can speculate on the hard-earned cumulative environmental knowledge that enabled the group to survive or the nonmaterial artistic expressions that permitted it to enjoy doing so. However, several finds among the meager residue of the Los Pinos Phase possibly shed light on activities less fundamental than those employed in preparing internal body fuel and external body warmth. A few unembellished bone beads and several tablets on which red or green minerals for pigment had been crushed attest to the vanities of personal adornment and body painting. Two dog burials in which hapless canines had been severed in half and interred affirm the practice of ritualistic sacrifice.

The Navajo Reservoir archaeologists attempting to reconstruct Los Pinos Phase life placed it between A.D. 1 and 400. A combination of dating techniques such as archaeomagnetism, radiocarbon analysis, and ceramic stylistic variation has allowed a refinement in dating that for some researchers shortens the period to between A.D. 150 and 400. Statistical studies based on the number of occupied zones, square footage of structures, and probable size of extended familial units produced a population estimate of less than three hundred persons overall in the Los Pinos Phase. Probably some habitations were overlooked because of faint surface indications, and the average size of nuclear families may have been greater than the base figure of three-plus individuals used in the reservoir study. Nevertheless, individual generational numbers over two and a half centuries appear to have been small.

Most of the Los Pinos dwellings were isolated units where a family lived near the land it tried to tame and cultivate. Four concentrations of a half-dozen houses in close proximity may be antecedents to the later established pattern of settled Pueblo village life. These groupings may have been used and reused over time rather than as permanent villages. The cultural stage as a whole was part of a more extensive distribution of eastern Basketmaker II people ranging southward from the vicinity of Durango, along the Animas River valley, and southeast across green uplands to the Pine. Still further east, the twin pinnacles of Chimney and Companion rocks overlooked a river valley far removed from where the action was. It remained quiet and unviolated.

Meanwhile, back near the Navajo Dam locale, the Los Pinos population either gradually dwindled away or sharply declined in number. Over centuries their post-and-cobblestone houses slumped back to earth.

Sambrito Village being excavated during the summer of 1960. *Courtesy Museum of New Mexico.*

SAMBRITO PHASE (BASKETMAKER III)
CA. A.D. 600–700

With a cultural revitalization, people again reappeared on the banks of the San Juan, and they chose to settle in what would become the middle reaches of the modern reservoir just south of the Colorado–New Mexico state line. They obviously regarded the front edges of broad Pleistocene benches lining the river as suitable for dry farming. Moisture from subsurface water and summer rains was sufficient to nourish their gardens. Whether or not the newcomers may have been migrants moving out of the Mogollon Mountains several hundred miles to the south, as was originally postulated, they carried some important cultural traits associated with that region.

Among the new introductions was a house style in which basal walls were the sides of a pit. The incentive for builders equipped with nothing more that long stout sticks, baskets, and an enormous application of

53

Deep pithouse in Sambrito Village (Basketmaker III, Site LA 4169) on a terrace above the San Juan River at its former confluence with Sambrito Creek. A central hearth, wing walls, floor cists, and ventilator shaft are typical features for the period. This pithouse was part of an extensive occupation at the site extending from ca. A.D. 400 to 1000, with a Navajo use of the same locale probably in the 1700s. *Courtesy Museum of New Mexico.*

human muscle to burrow commodious round holes three to four feet down into stubborn rocky soil is not as hard to explain as it might seem. First, southern influence may have been infiltrating northward about the seventh century; more important, the adoption of the true pithouse had a practical ecological basis. The tree cover needed for wall logs was thin to absent in many places on the Colorado Plateau, but dirt was everywhere. Furthermore, digging-stick excavation actually may have been no more laborious than felling timber with cumbersome stone implements or fire and then manually transporting the heavy beams to construction localities. And, as people in arid environments worldwide have discovered, earthen architecture tends to be cool in summer and warm in winter. With most living activities assumed to have taken place out of doors, houses primarily were havens from inclement weather or for sleeping.

The first San Juan pithouses were relatively small and shallow, with the same interior characteristics as the earlier Los Pinos log-and-cobble-stone structures. Floors were mud plastered, sloped up cuplike to meet mud-plastered walls, and were riddled with various storage holes, post depressions, pot rests, and a central hearth. Benches for storage or for sleeping were cut from pit sides. Ventilation to allow fresh air in and stale air out was achieved by a vertical slot opening at ground level gouged out of the encircling earth. In small houses, access and egress was achieved by means of a ladder through a smoke hole over the central fire basin; in larger dwellings, a ramp from ground level into an entry antechamber was used. Roofs probably were low and truncated; timbers leaned up against a square center beam frame to form the slanted upper walls of the pit, and the whole affair was covered with a thick layer of earth.

Even though exterior wall construction was modified, the preference for a circular floor plan and the general pattern of usage remained the same as it had been in the previous centuries of semisettled life. Parents, children, and possibly a grandparent all shared one enclosed living space. Probably two or three generations of related families were accommodated in more spacious units. In some cases, these greater structures may also have been gathering places for integrative social or religious group functions. Outside was an associated array of underground cists, which excavator Frank Eddy interpreted as baking ovens. At one locality, forty-five such subterranean undercut pits were discovered. They were found accidentally when a bulldozer operator scraped the ground to reveal an unsuspected complex of pit mouths crowded into a confined area. Several of the so-called ovens were found to have doubled as convenient crypts for human remains and the carcasses of

Overview of a concentration of Sambrito Phase (Basketmaker III) fired cists excavated in 1962. They were dug into a spur of land on the east bank of the San Juan River half a mile above its former junction with the Piedra River. Contemporary and later houses were in the vicinity. *Courtesy Museum of New Mexico.*

dogs severed in half. Even in this Stone Age culture, few were foolish enough to dig with a stick when it was unnecessary.

A second major addition to the cultural inventory was pottery. The ideas for its manufacture are thought to have passed along from central Mexico to reach the Mogollones, whose homeland straddled what are now the international Mexican-U.S. borderlands of Arizona and New Mexico, about the time of Christ. From that place and time, the concept of pottery making reached outward in ever-widening ripples and was adopted by diverse peoples, who at the same time were embracing sedentism, for which pottery was appropriate. The earliest pottery samples from this second period of San Juan occupation are a crude but polished ware. Because it is brownish in color, researchers earlier speculated either that pottery was traded from southern Mogollon to northern Anasazi along some commercial network or that Mogollon potters may

Small, undecorated, brown utility pottery recovered from the Sambrito Phase (Basketmaker III) type site: a) bowl; b) spouted bowl; c and d) jars. *Courtesy Museum of New Mexico*.

have been among those who took up homesteads on the San Juan. Recent reanalysis shows that local alluvial clays rich in iron content and a firing process then used by novice potters that allowed limited oxidation explained the brown coloration, rather than any outside influence or artisans. The vessels often were begun in a basket. Coils of clay then were added upward and welded together through finger pressure and scraping, then smoothed by a hard-edged object, perhaps a chunk of dried gourd rind or a piece of broken pottery. Basket impressions were retained on some vessel bottoms.

Undoubtedly pottery greatly facilitated the household chores of storage, cooking, and eating. For convenience, water could be kept in the dwellings. Without glaze for waterproofing, some evaporation through the walls of storage jars occurred, but this process kept the contents of the vessels cool. Dry foodstuffs could be kept in small containers without requiring another cist in the floor. The availability of heat-resistant, semi-impervious receptacles promoted new culinary procedures. After hundreds of years of a dry diet of raw plants, parched seeds, roasted corn, and rare bits of skewered meat grilled over a smoky fire, more liquid preparations, such as gruels, stews, and herbal teas, must have been gastronomic delights. It is noteworthy that the growing of beans, a final cultigen added to the standard triad of prehistoric Southwestern domesticates and whose preparation necessitated boiling, was somewhat contemporaneous with the introduction of pottery.

The first vessel forms were small, round-bottomed jars, some with necks, and bowls having indrawn orifices. These could well have been cook pots that would have nestled down into an open hearth and whose contours helped to hold in heat. Fired clay items in divergent shapes were for other purposes. These included circular spindle whorls used in weaving and objects, such as a bird effigy and short conical pipes, with possible ceremonial functions.

A complement of stone and bone implements was retrieved. Among these artifacts were small stone projectile points suitable for tipping arrows, fragments of juniper bark matting, and scraps of basketry. Particularly intriguing were a few ornaments, including pendants, beads, and bracelets, made from Pacific shells. With the source of the shells hundreds of miles away from this ancient dry-land outpost on the San

Juan, the jewelry confirmed the existence of long-distance trade channels. Finished items were special enough to be fitting offerings for the dead.

The archaeologist in charge of these excavations judged the remains to be from the Basketmaker III horizon. In accordance with the San Juan chronology developed by project personnel, he called this the "Sambrito Phase." Basing his opinion on a combination of stratigraphic and ceramic dating methods and a few radiocarbon dates, he believed it fell within a three-hundred-year interval, from A.D. 400 to 700. Consequently, in his opinion the Sambrito Phase represented a vital connecting link in the local continuum between the Basketmaker and Pueblo time frames. If so, then there was no gap in occupation in the district, as was believed prior to the Navajo Dam archaeological work.

Not all colleagues agree with this assessment. One opinion is that some of the dates are not relevant and that there was a hiatus of perhaps two hundred years between the Los Pinos and Sambrito phases. Another is that the Los Pinos and Sambrito phases were more compressed in time than the reservoir crew would have them and that they overlapped to such an extent as to be one evolutionary period rather than two distinct ones. The estimate of a mere fifty to sixty individuals living over a span of three centuries in just seven sites of uncertain contemporaneity also casts doubt on the validity of this phase. However, most Sambrito sites experienced subsequent occupations, which may have obscured some underriding Sambrito materials. There well may have been a more extensive population than the survey actually identified.

ROSA PHASE (EARLY PUEBLO I)
CA. A.D. 700–850

Some time in the early eighth century there was a land rush to the upper San Juan. The archaeological team found a string of sites that had been lived in at that time stretching the entire distance of the proposed reservoir. The heaviest concentration of pithouse ruins was just south of the New Mexico–Colorado state line, where the landforms were not as rugged as those closer to the dam site. For the first time the Anasazi had discovered the broad flat valley at the confluence of the Piedra and San Juan rivers. Estimates are that the population increased twentyfold over that of the preceding Sambrito Phase. Even so, with 225 individuals per generation spread over a varied tract of land thirty-four miles long, congestion was not a problem. However, this population estimate may be too low.

Where did these people come from? The most logical source is the Gobernador drainage flowing into the San Juan network from the southeast. Work there just before World War II demonstrated a flourishing late-Basketmaker III–Pueblo I occupation, in many respects not unlike that on the San Juan. Tree-ring analysis established construction dates of the Gobernador in the late 700s through the 800s for a period the archaeologist termed the Rosa Phase. At the same time, a notable augmentation of Anasazi numbers occurred in other sectors of the northern periphery of the Colorado Plateau. It would seem that settled existence supported by a growing emphasis upon agriculture led to a prehistoric baby boom.

A second question is: Why did the Anasazi move into a region that apparently held little appeal earlier? One reason may have been a simple overflow from a nearby center of development, where desirable lands were at a premium. Because the Gobernador district had no permanent rivers, perhaps the perennial waters of the San Juan and the broader floodplains in the upper reservoir pool area acquired new value with increased gardening. Also, some of the Gobernador settlements were encircled by defensive post stockades; the potential for raiding may have prompted movement into more secure canyonlands.

The original areal survey and subsequent excavation of sixteen Rosa Phase sites in the reservoir preserve showed the dominant settlement pattern to be isolated single pithouses, some away from the riverine settings, with a few grouped into hamlets. There were a greater number of units at each village than in the Sambrito Phase, as required by the presence of more inhabitants. The semisubterranean dwellings were larger than those of the Sambritos, dug deeper although still relatively shallow, and had more structured ventilator shafts and full or partial benches. A few boasted a *sipapu,* or ceremonial floor opening to the spirit

Excavations at late Rosa to Arboles phases (Pueblo I–early Pueblo II) Sanchez
Site situated near the former juncture of the San Juan and Piedra rivers. The
Hispanic community of Arboles, Colorado, in the background now lies
beneath the waters of the Navajo Reservoir. *Courtesy Museum of New Mexico.*

world, possibly indicating that, in addition to being domestic houses,
these were places of cult activities. Some homeowners had had enough
of digging-stick excavation and built rectangular surface rooms of jacal
for living and storage. Refuse either was thrown around the premises,
most typically on the downhill slopes, or dumped into the nearest
flowing water. In randomly scattering shelters and trash, the locals
deviated from the custom of their contemporaries in other districts.
Whether that was by choice, laziness, or ignorance of what was expected
is a tantalizing question.

Although some brown pottery continued to be produced, the gray
wares that were to characterize Anasazi output for the next six hundred
years made their appearance in considerable abundance. Earthenwares
had become indispensable furnishings. The gray base color resulted from
the firing process: pots were baked over smothered flames, which reduced the amount of oxygen in the atmosphere. It is not known why

potters chose to follow this method, but it made Anasazi pottery unique in the ancient Southwest.

Most vessels were hard and rough-textured. Those intended for storage or cooking increased in size over what they had been in Sambrito times and were left plain. However, unobliterated coils of necks of some jars reinforced a vulnerable part of the pot, at the same time adding a decorative touch. This neck-banding became a hallmark of Pueblo I. Open serving bowls were also made, and with them came the introduction of crude painted decorations. A pigment that fired black was derived from boiling down parts of plants, such as the tansy mustard and Rocky Mountain beeweed. This process obviously could not have been undertaken prior to the existence of receptacles in which to cook liquids and solids together — in short, because the Rosa Phase housewives had pots, they then could decorate them. A less frequently used pigment was made from a pulverized lead mineral. This fluxed, turned greenish, and partially vitrified under low temperatures.

Some pottery traits, such as the green lead-glaze pigment, were generally out of date elsewhere by the eighth or ninth centuries. The production of gray ware, the use of painted decoration, the application of slip, and the making of open bowls and other forms seem to have become part of the technology of these artisans later than in other parts of the Pueblo I sphere. This lagging development underscores the marginal geographical situation in which this society operated. There would always be a backwoodsiness about the upper San Juan Anasazi.

The archaeological record indicates that Rosa Phase participants were increasingly committed to horticultural pursuits. Campsites on the floodplains were interpreted as places where farmers stayed while tending fields. Numerous hafted stone axes were thought to have helped clear land and build houses. Fewer projectile points and stone knives were recovered from the principal sites, a sign that hunting was not as important as it had been. More manos and metates for grinding and more vessels and baskets for storage reflected increased production of foodstuffs needing to be processed and stowed away. Rosa Phase Anasazi had culturally adapted to their environment.

Their existence remained a hardscrabble one. Still, a general cultural enrichment is demonstrated in a greater variety of stone, bone, and shell objects, some of which were imported from outside the immediate region. A few luxury items were present, such as hairpins, whistles, and shell and gilsonite jewelry. Conspicuous consumption was occasionally displayed in burials, where a cache of two dozen pieces of pottery might be placed in a single grave for an individual with a degree of social standing.

With a modicum of success in horticulture, the Anasazi quite surely became concerned about assuring its continuation. That meant religion. From the time men planted the first seeds to bring on the Neolithic Revolution, they fretted about the weather and felt at the mercy of a myriad of little-understood natural forces. The rains that did not come, the hail that wounded gardens, the hot winds that seared the soil, and the late frosts that turned seedlings brown and limp were seen as the actions of supernatural beings who had to be placated with ritual offerings and prayers. The few material clues to that side of early Pueblo thought are some pottery effigy figures of ducks and fish — both associated with the crucial natural element of water — clay cloud-blower pipes, and stone corn-goddess symbols. The bizarre slaughter of man's best friend, a trait also observed in the Gobernador remains, seems to have been done for other reasons.

Despite whatever rites may have been performed around the *sipapus*, the Rosa Phase Anasazi were threatened with a natural disaster at the middle of the ninth century. One of the recurring cycles of riverine down-cutting, which for eons had chewed the Colorado Plateau and spit it out in the Gulf of California, began again. Because of major shifts in climatic patterns, the San Juan River steadily became more deeply entrenched in its middle sections, where the gradient was greatest. That, in turn, drained away the subsurface water that nourished tender roots of Anasazi corn, beans, and squash. The lands on which those plants grew were left high and dry, and surrounding terrain suffered a reduction in vegetational cover.

One can visualize the elders, squatting on their haunches around the hearths, debating what to do. What they did was what they had done before and would do again: they moved. Demographic shifts were a way of life for the Anasazi as a means of coping with a country only marginally suitable for agriculture. If the nutrients of thin soil were exhausted or precipitation patterns changed where they were, the Anasazi farmers found another place to try again. Many of the thousands of former settlements that dot the northern Southwest probably were lived in for only a decade or two. The forced relocations may not have been particularly traumatic. Although it meant starting over, generally no great distance was involved, and the neighbors, houses, their arrangements on the landscape, and apparatus for living remained much the same. The Anasazi householder was not bothered with transporting a plethora of unnecessary things.

So it was that around A.D. 850 the lower ten and a half miles of the reservoir district were abandoned as the San Juan Anasazi migrated to greener pastures. They could not head south because there was a dearth of good farmland in the barren slopes of the Chaco Plateau. To the west a heavy population along the La Plata drainage already had usurped the best areas. Northward the frost belt fronting the San Juan Mountains presented too many subsistence obstacles. So they went upriver ahead of the entrenchment, keeping to a riverine/low upland environment and becoming further isolated from their contemporaries in the lower San Juan Basin.

PIEDRA PHASE (LATE PUEBLO I)
CA. A.D. 850–950

Coincident with the progress of the Navajo Reservoir excavations, archaeologists came to accept the use of heavy earth-moving equipment to clear sites of sterile overburden accumulated through centuries of deposition. Consequently, a backhoe, operated by an archaeologist fully aware of the cultural composition of the sites being examined, skinned off the crusty surface and dug bucket-sized trenches through promising sectors to provide a profile of the zone. Occasionally the backhoe exposed subsurface dwellings that were undetected from the surface. A great amount of time and effort was saved by this mechanical aid. Once the peek beneath the earth's rind was afforded, researchers quickly decided whether or not the site might add new data to fit into their

long-term study goals. When the decision was made to continue excavation, crews from the local Hispanic communities took to their shovels
and trowels, just as they had done in Roberts's day.

In the ninth and tenth centuries, the lifestyle of the greater numbers
of upper San Juan Anasazi became more fixed into a static highland
tradition distinctive from that evolving at Chaco Canyon to the south
or in the Mesa Verde region to the northwest. Most peoples of this era,
called the Piedra Phase by the excavators, continued to live in single-
unit pithouses of several styles dispersed along the terraces above the
river, but there were more of them per square mile than previously. At
the mouth of the Piedra River where the stream meandered through rich
silts, forty sites were noted, twenty-nine of which were occupied during
the Piedra Phase, or late Pueblo I. A preference for utilization of Recent
terraces rather than higher Pleistocene benches confirms the need to
tap lower water levels. The walls of some Piedra Phase pithouses were
reinforced by poles to forestall slumping, but otherwise their style
differed little from that of their ancestors. The Piedrans constructed one
or a linear series of rectangular jacal rooms on the ground surface nearby.
The fact that some were outfitted with fire hearths shows them to have
been used for living rather than for storage. The jacal rooms generally
had cobble or sandstone foundations and occasional cobblestone paving
to discourage burrowing rodents. Trash was thrown in a heap off to one
side. In general, the remains in the lower Piedra Valley resembled those
that Roberts had explored thirty years earlier in the northern portion of
the valley.

Because of the gradual movement upriver, several villages that had
been inhabited in earlier times expanded in size. The largest, located on
the west bank at the confluence of the San Juan River and Sambrito
Creek, consisted of ninety-one identifiable units. Judging from architectural features and datable ceramics, nineteen pithouses, thirteen surface
structures, and five exterior pits were left from the Piedra Phase resi-
dency. That appears to have been the peak period of use of the community, because during the next epoch only a single pithouse was lived in.
By the early 1000s it, too, was vacated. Eight hundred years later Navajos
moved in to erect four forked-stick hogans adjacent to the almost

obliterated pit depressions. These more recent inhabitants undoubtedly salvaged surviving useful artifacts discarded by their predecessors.

An enrichment in the sociopsychological life of the Piedrans may explain the digging of an extra large pithouse in each locality having a concentration of smaller structures. The grandest of all had more than fifteen hundred square feet of floor space. The roof probably was supported by six large posts arranged in a circular pattern about the floor. An encircling bench and an absence of floor features were notable. These "super-pithouses" likely served as community centers for the village and outlying satellite homes. Based upon indirect evidence, some usage of a religious nature can be assumed. For example, clay effigy figures of fish or waterfowl, a cone-shaped stone regarded as a corn-goddess fetish, and presumed medicine kits containing exotic rocks or fossils may have been cult goods for ceremonies held in such places. Having large ceremonial or gathering rooms as part of a settlement cluster was the rule rather than the exception in most contemporaneous Anasazi quarters located on the eastern and northern Colorado Plateau. The Navajo Reservoir archaeologists called theirs Shabik'eschee kivas, after a Great Kiva dug in Chaco Canyon by Roberts. However, the huge pit structures of the Piedra Phase lacked any direct ties to Chaco itself; they merely represented a widespread sharing of a cultural phenomenon.

Although substantial finds of corn cobs and kernels, squash rinds, and beans suggest successful harvests, and although faunal remains can be interpreted as discards from fruitful hunting forays, the general economy may not have been flourishing. Cultural growth stagnated. Despite some refinements in stone tools and increased mastery of the craft of pottery making, there were few major additions to the repertoire of material things. Trade goods were limited. Moreover, the Piedra Phase was a period of reduced rainfall and shorter growing seasons. These factors, added to the continued headward erosion of the river, probably made suitable farmland scarce and harvests uncertain. Conflicts may have erupted within the group over food supplies and perhaps over the ineffectiveness of religious leaders in assuring their abundance. In addition, the resident population may have clashed with outsiders, who also might have been affected by adverse conditions.

There is some confirmation of turbulent times on the San Juan during the ninth and tenth centuries. Several of the larger villages were surrounded by stockades of upright posts wedged into position by stones. Although one opinion is that the stockades were meant to confine turkeys, they may have reflected a perceived need for defense. A clue to trouble on the San Juan came from one pithouse that contained the long bones and skulls of twelve individuals. The long bones had been fleshed and opened while green, with interior marrow scraped out. After being cannibalized, the bones were tossed on the floor and the house above set on fire. In other dwellings human skeletal remains also had been incinerated. Just as on Stollsteimer Mesa, many structures had burned. Certainly strife brought on by extreme desperation is a possibility.

ARBOLES PHASE (EARLY PUEBLO II)
CA. A.D. 950–1050

The northeastern Anasazi may have fought each other, but they could not fight Mother Nature. According to one interpretation, year by year the San Juan River hungrily ate into its bed and borders, further lowering the critical water table and devouring potential farmlands. Even runoff-water farming, wherein fields were cultivated at the outlets of channels or arroyos, proved risky. A conflicting view is that about A.D. 1000 the San Juan River valley experienced high water tables and aggradation that brought on flooding of the valley floor. Regardless of the underlying causes, people slowly migrated upriver and gathered together into small communities. For a century fewer than several hundred persons remained near the mouth of the Piedra and eastward along the base of Sandoval Mesa, which forms the north cliff of the San Juan River.

The Arboles Phase people, or Early Pueblo II in the traditional classification, continued to reside in the pithouses that had become customary for the region. On occasion they also erected linear rows of surface rooms made of sandstone slabs laid horizontally in thick beds of mud, the first attempts at masonry on the upper San Juan. They were what Roberts called "Type C construction" on Stollsteimer Mesa. These units were floored with cobbles. Other surface structures were of jacal over cobble foundations. Excavators uncovered some evidence for temporary brush *ramadas* which could have been used for outdoor workplaces. In pottery manufacture, the participants of the Arboles Phase adopted use of white background slip for painted vessels and relatively infrequent corrugation on exteriors for gray wares. The latter were pinched spirally, a distinctive surface treatment. The vessel forms to which it was applied were baglike and different from anything in the rest of the northern San Juan area.

ANASAZI UPRIVER

In the late 1960s and early 1970s there was a postscript to the Navajo Reservoir archaeological project. E. Charles Adams, then a graduate student at the University of Colorado, undertook a study of Anasazi settlement patterns along the San Juan drainages upriver from the lake created by the Navajo Dam. The area encompassed 45,000 square acres of the Southern Ute Indian Reservation in Archuleta County southeast of Chimney and Companion rocks and north of the San Juan River. Adams confirmed a cultural expression comparable to that within the reservoir pool and tabulated 147 sites ranging in date over a three-hundred-year period from A.D. 750 to 1050. From about A.D. 850 on, these proved to be remains resulting from ecological pressures downriver. Over time, these pressures forced northeasterly migration toward the foothills of the Rocky Mountains, where Cat Creek Ridge formed a natural 8,000-foot-high boundary rimmed with sandstone.

Adams's work coincided with the inception of the computer age in Southwestern archaeology. He focused on statistical analyses of data in order to understand why and how the Anasazi settled in and adapted to diverse environmental niches within this locality and ultimately forsook them. Through these means Adams concluded that all the usual explanations for settlement — i.e., carrying capacity of lands as a result of agricultural modifications, cold air drainage into narrow valleys, population growth and consequent stresses, social, economic, or political activities, transportation routes, natural defensive features, and the need or potential for new foodstuffs — were by themselves too narrow in focus. All, however, likely contributed in some way to site distribution.

The carrying capacity of what Adams termed the lower Piedra district (although the Piedra River valley was not included) in any one phase was 308 individuals. Using an arbitrary figure taken from ethnographic analogy (i.e., comparison with modern Native American communities) of six individuals per pithouse, he found that at no time were there more persons present than the district could support. Adams estimated a population during the Rosa Phase (A.D. 750–850) of 210 persons, or one-third less than the maximum. They lived in dispersed single-family pithouses in riverine terrace settings near arable lands, and their development was coeval to that on the lower San Juan; they were not there because of the misfortunes that later came to pass in the Navajo Reservoir district. Horticulture still being a part-time affair, these Rosans had little need for many additional storage facilities.

The Piedra Phase (A.D. 850–950) saw a peak district population of 258 persons, who continued to dwell in pithouses but often clustered them in the uplands, where higher elevation and greater precipitation meant annual soil moisture was more evenly distributed and the principal crop of maize had a better chance of flourishing. Typically these Piedrans also built jacal or limited-function surface structures in locations where wild foodstuffs could be procured, stored, and processed. Some of these settlers had indigenous roots, but others migrated into the district because of environmental changes downriver.

During the Arboles Phase (A.D. 950–1050), the number of people present declined to an estimated 120 because of movement out of the district resulting from a decrease in the amount of tillable land. The actual size of the pithouse settlements increased as people came together to more fully exploit what riverine locations there were. Jacal surface units were placed next to plots of farmlands, enabling individuals to claim and more efficiently work them.

Ultimately, environmental conditions deteriorated to the point that further adaptations in order to maintain cultural stability were no longer possible. Beginning a little after A.D. 1000, a migration out of the main upper San Juan territory began. Those who went southeast across the

Continental Divide in New Mexico likely formed the population out of which the Gallina culture evolved several centuries later. Those who drifted ten or eleven miles up the Piedra Valley linked with contemporary Chimney Rock communities, the evidence of which Jeancon and Roberts first used in 1921 to launch regional archaeology. They formed a stranded enclave on headlands in the shadow of the rocks.

ANASAZI EXPOSED

A quarter of a century after the Navajo Reservoir archaeological project terminated, a second chance to reexamine some of the submerged antiquities unexpectedly arose. In 1987, when the dam was being repaired, the water level was drastically reduced to the point where prehistoric sites once again were exposed and a human skull at one of them caught the attention of boaters on the lake. The Bureau of Reclamation contacted Complete Archaeological Service Associates of Cortez, Colorado, to recover what eroding human remains were evident and conduct salvage excavations where warranted.

The skull came from a burned pit at the lower edge of a clay ridge that had extended underwater from the shore near the junction of the San Juan and Piedra rivers. The archaeologists assumed the location to be the Basketmaker III Oven Site excavated by Frank Eddy in 1962, where he had noted an unusually dense concentration of subterranean cists. Because fires obviously had reddened their interiors, Eddy concluded that they had been used for roasting animal or plant foods. No remaining particles of those foods were recovered, however, nor were there any associated fire-cracked rocks that might have been used to conduct heat.

Nancy and Larry Hammack, owners of the contract archaeological firm involved in 1987, and their crew determined that the newly exposed pit was one of a complex of an additional twenty-three similar constructions situated upslope from the Oven Site. The pits were identical to those at the Oven Site, making a total of sixty-eight known cists in the immediate vicinity. They acknowledged a strong probability that others

The 1989 excavation of storage cists at the Oven Site (LA 4169) first examined in 1962. *Courtesy Complete Archaeological Service Associates.*

are there in many suitable spots along the former river terraces, which are no longer visible.

The cone-shaped pits were gouged by digging sticks about three feet down into a deep bank of clay, which formed the feature walls. The floors had diameters of three to nine feet and were flat. Pit mouths were restricted and had been sealed with thin, large, worked sandstone slabs that, after abandonment, had slumped into the interior fill. All but one of the pits had been burned prior to being used, which hardened the clay walls to an imperviousness sufficient to thwart rodent and insect activity and moisture seepage. The sandstone covers showed no comparable fire reddening. Taking all these factors into consideration, the Hammacks viewed the pits as terra-cotta subterranean storage silos rather than ovens.

Whether the burned pits were used for cooking or for warehousing, their number emphasizes great success in farming and foraging and indirectly hints at a larger residential population than was first postulated. A dating technique called archaeomagnetism (wherein iron particles in

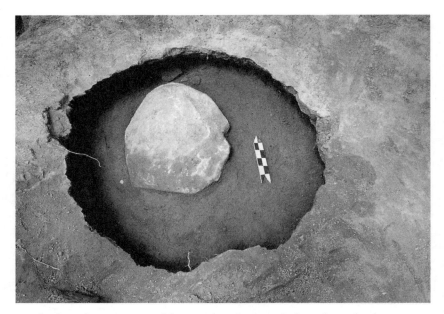

Looking down into one of the complex of sixty-eight large, burned, subterranean cists at the Oven Site dating from the seventh century. The stone was a roughly shaped lid, the surrounding mouth of the cist having eroded and fallen into the pit. *Courtesy Complete Archaeological Service Associates.*

burned clay are measured for their alignment with known positions through time of the magnetic north pole) worked out in the years between the Navajo Reservoir archaeological project and the recent salvage work confirms construction in the late sixth or early seventh centuries. The Sambrito Phase span defined by Eddy thereby is verified.

At a later time, the pits were used as tombs. Single burials were found in five of them — it was the skull from one such grave that alarmed the Bureau of Reclamation in 1987. Bodies were laid out on pit floors and covered with fill dirt rich with the remains of wild and domestic plants. Associated ceramic offerings were indicative of the late Sambrito Phase.

To determine whether other sites within the pool area were being similarly impacted by wave action or fluctuation of water levels, the crew took to a pontoon boat to survey the shoreline. Eerily, after being sunk for so many years, stone rings around sixteen-hundred-year-old pit structures reemerged from their watery grave and were clearly visible on slimy mud flats. Around them, heavy stone objects that had been left where found in the 1960s were still in place, but all lighter sheet trash and spoil dirt taken out of the excavation area had washed away. No further skeletal materials surfaced.

Now all that is left of these Anasazi and their material accomplishments is safely back underwater. The lake impounded by the great earthen Navajo Dam has drowned the ghost towns of perhaps a thousand years of Anasazi history. Yet the cultural record might never have been so fully reconstructed had it not been for the modern water needs of the Navajo Nation and ultimately the conglomerates of Phoenix and Los Angeles.

(a) View over stabilized walls of the Chimney Rock pueblo toward the modern fire tower and the two pinnacles in the background. *Courtesy Jim Fuge.*

(b) Sunrise over Chimney Rock. *Courtesy Jim Fuge*.

(c) View of Chimney Rock from southwest flank of the San Juan Mountains. *Courtesy Jim Fuge*.

(d) The trail from the ruins of the Chimney Rock pueblo runs west down a ridge of the Chimney Rock cuesta toward the Piedra River valley in the distance. *Courtesy Jim Fuge.*

(e) Aerial view of the Chimney Rock pueblo. *Courtesy Jim Fuge*.

(f) Aerial view of the excavated Chimney Rock pueblo roomblock and two kivas. *Courtesy Tom McMurray.*

(g) Aerial view to southeast over the Chimney Rock pueblo, the pinnacles, and San Juan Mountains in the distance. *Courtesy Jim Fuge*.

(h) The two Chimney Rock pinnacles from which the site derives its name. *Courtesy Tom McMurray.*

4

ANASAZI IN THE BACKWATER

For nearly fifty years the excavated portions of the Chacoan pueblo on the uppermost crest of the Chimney Rock mesa lay bare. Decay began almost immediately upon the departure of the diggers from the State Historical and Natural History Society. Rains pelting against the exposed masonry slowly dissolved the mud mortar. Freezing and thawing pried veneer from its rubble core backing. As a result, large sections of walls collapsed into heaps of sandstone blocks and were covered with windblown dirt and tumbleweeds. As Jeancon had warned in 1922, a vulnerable Anasazi ruin was becoming ever more ruinous.

Finally, in 1968, administrators of the San Juan National Forest initiated efforts to reclaim this neglected cultural resource before it was too late. They signed a contract with the Mesa Verde Research Center, a field station of the Department of Anthropology at the University of Colorado, to clean up the derelict houseblock and excavate associated sites on the cuesta. An archaeological preserve of 6.12 square miles was to be set aside for public inspection. Beginning the ensuing summer and continuing for the two following seasons, teams of student archaeologists under the direction of Frank W. Eddy, who had been a primary field researcher in the Navajo Reservoir Archaeological Project, toiled on the Chimney Rock mesa. They cleared formerly dug sections of the large structure and excavated one room, the previously untouched part of the east kiva, and the east and south courtyards adjacent to the building. As they finished, a crew of Navajo workers specially trained in ruin-stabilization procedures reset stones, capped walls, and tried to secure the house's future well-being. Their supplies of sand and cement were

Chimney Rock pueblo as it appeared before 1970s' stabilization. *Courtesy San Juan National Forest.*

brought to the site by helicopter, and a water line for mixing mortar was run up the mesa.

Additionally, the researchers examined four complexes of structures lower on the mesa: the so-called guardhouse on a spine of rocky land below the primary pueblo and three others near the terminus of a road the Forest Service was building up the south escarpment. They also made a survey of the entire precinct down to the waterways on three sides of the landform in order to determine the kind and extent of prehistoric occupation that had occurred and its probable temporal relationship to the crowning pueblo at the base of the twin pinnacles. This gathering of data has allowed a series of related studies that continue to the present.

To first consider the story revealed on the upper Chimney Rock mesa is like reading the last chapter of a book before working through the preliminary digitations of the plot. Anasazi pioneers laid the groundwork for later developments on the Chimney Rock mesa during the second half of the ninth century or a bit later, moving out of the main San Juan River artery because of untenable conditions and making their way up the Piedra Valley. Frank Roberts encountered evidence of their arrival and settlement on terraces lining the tributary Piedra River and on the

Collapsed room walls of Chimney Rock pueblo prior to stabilization. *Courtesy San Juan National Forest.*

Excavators trench rubble accumulated over an earth-paved courtyard along the south wall of Chimney Rock pueblo (Site 5AA83). *Courtesy University of Colorado.*

Stollsteimer Mesa that fronted the river on the east. They clustered detached and contiguous rooms around large man-made depressions, which Roberts thought were merely borrow pits for mud mortar but others now suspect may have resulted from caved-in community pit structures. He reported no single-unit pithouses on Stollsteimer Mesa but considered the jacal rooms to have provided year-round shelter and storage.

Just prior to the 1970s' work on Chimney Rock mesa, a group of university students under the direction of Robert H. Lister conducted

West kiva of the Chimney Rock pueblo, showing condition of walls prior to
1970s stabilization. *Courtesy University of Colorado.*

an archaeological survey of adjacent Southern Ute Indian Reservation
lands. This survey included parts of the upper Piedra Valley, Stollsteimer
Mesa, Lake Capote at the eastern foot of Chimney Rock, and the
highlands west of the Piedra River. The surveyors encountered the
by-then familiar pithouse depressions, rock alignments of circular or
rectangular rooms, burned adobe clods and posts left from jacal structures, rock art, and areas without architectural features but covered with
stone flakes discarded during projectile point and tool manufacture.
These signs of former human presence were at elevations centering on
7,000 feet. The team also excavated a Pueblo I pithouse in the vicinity

Stabilized walls of rooms and west kiva. *Courtesy San Juan National Forest.*

of the Southern Ute agency at Ignacio on the Pine River. It conformed in style and content to the finds of coeval sites throughout the northeastern San Juan region. More recent surveys have reaffirmed a cultural sequence across the wedge of uplands between the Pine and Piedra rivers comparable to that along the San Juan River, with a notable withdrawal toward the northeast.

Once the University of Colorado team began its survey of the Chimney Rock Archeological Area of the national forest, it found extensive Piedra Phase (late Pueblo I) occupation on terraces bordering the river. Pithouses of several sizes accompanied by jacal surface structures laid out in bars or L- or U-shapes were characteristic. Excavation is needed to know whether they were deep or shallow.

These various undertakings confirmed that as population pressures increased throughout the tenth century because of the influx of people dislocated from the primary San Juan drainage to the south, a major movement to the very head of the Piedra Valley occurred. This migration brought the Anasazi to the environmental limits for their maize-

Trail, or causeway, down the cuesta spine from the Chimney Rock pueblo toward the guardhouse ruin. *Courtesy San Juan National Forest.*

Archaeologists clear overgrowth from a mounded site (5AA92) about to be destroyed in 1970–1971 by road construction up the south side of the Chimney Rock mesa. *Courtesy University of Colorado.*

based horticulture and into a ponderosa pine, piñon, and juniper vegetational zone. Elevations ranged from 6,400 to 6,700 feet in the floodplain and on the benches along the south and north slopes of Chimney Rock mesa, where lower temperatures prevailed than in the regions from which they had come. Moreover, cold air settled in the relatively narrow upper Piedra Valley, and the prominences on the east and west horizons blocked the sun's warming rays except at midday. These factors were responsible for a shortened growing season for maize that hovered precariously around the 110 to 120 days necessary for maturation. A slight climatic change meant probable crop loss. However, there were advantages to the new setting: a sandy loam soil suitable for the raising of maize; broad, relatively flat areas that could be cleared and cultivated; a permanent water supply in the river and increased precipitation because of the proximity of the high mountains; reduced evapotranspiration, keeping soil moist; and accessible resources such as timber, stone, clay, and wild foodstuffs.

Northwesterly view from the crest of the Chimney Rock mesa toward the upper end of the Piedra Valley. Terraces descending to the river were densely occupied by Anasazi of the Piedra and Arboles phases (late Pueblo I–early Pueblo II). *Courtesy San Juan National Forest.*

Life for the tenth-century Arboles Phase (early Pueblo II) Anasazi on the upper Piedra proved satisfactory. Their numbers multiplied. Particularly on the toe of the Chimney Rock mesa overlooking the juncture of the Piedra River and Devil Creek, they congregated together in villages composed of pithouses and small surface units of a few adjoining rooms built of various combinations of jacal, cobbles, and sandstone slabs. Several towers in addition to those explored by Jeancon and Roberts were present, as were assorted roasting pits and storage cists lined with sandstone. Without excavation, it is impossible to know if the numerous large depressions near these identifiable structures were remains of community ceremonial rooms, oversized domestic pithouses, or a mixture of both.

Just as the architectural conventions that evolved over centuries of occupation on the upper San Juan remained relatively constant, so too

Unexcavated sites on the terraces above the upper Piedra River, of probable early Pueblo II age, appear as scatters of stone slabs from fallen walls. *Courtesy San Juan National Forest.*

did those of material culture. The comparatively small but varied yield of artifacts included a few stone objects such as manos, metates, mortars, axes, polishing and abrading stones, lap anvils, pot lids, scrapers, gravers, hammers, and drills made from local river cobbles. Projectile points were common enough to suggest that hunting was an important activity. Pottery was represented primarily by a limited number of restorable gray vessels and a random assortment of fragments from others. Black-on-white potsherds came almost exclusively from simple bowls. Occasional corrugated texturing on utility jars and broad-lined designs on service vessels are probably signs of a widespread sharing of basic ideas among all northern San Juan Anasazi rather than direct influence from any one specific source, such as Mesa Verde.

The picture that emerges from analysis of Piedran architecture and material culture is that these were ultraconservative people who moved out of the reservoir area and became increasingly cut off from meaningful contact with Anasazi living elsewhere on the Colorado Plateau who

Vessel shape and surface texturing identify this utility vessel as a type named Payan Corrugated, whose styling was to continue into later occupation of the Gallina area of north central New Mexico. *Courtesy Marcia Truell Newren.*

might have brought innovations to the local lifestyle. Such interaction as did exist took place with those who lived due south of the San Juan in the Gobernador area and followed a comparable cultural pattern. Trade items, other than a very small amount of obsidian from the Jemez Mountains and farther south in New Mexico, are scarce. Mountain nomads of undetermined affiliation may have exchanged hides and wild foods for pottery.

Those wild foods, whether traded for or gathered by hand, expanded the diet beyond the corn and bean cultigens. Especially in hard times, the biologically rich mountain environment prompted a dramatic return to a hunting-and-gathering subsistence base more characteristic of the opening eras of the Anasazi continuum. Modern flotation methods, in which buckets of soil are subjected to water separation to extract fossilized pollen, indicate that rose hips, serviceberries, chokecherries, wild currants, sunflower seeds, and prickly pears were gathered in season. A few wild species, such as lamb's-quarters, probably were allowed to colonize garden plots. Curiously, the piñon nut–juniper berry–oak acorn assemblage typically a part of the native plant communities was not found by paleoenvironmentalists in the retrieved materials. This absence probably was due to a sampling problem.

As for hunting, elk, mule deer, bear, mountain sheep, and other large game were bagged. Bones of smaller animals further indicate a diversified meat component to the diet, as well as an abundance of bone resources for tools and adornment, and furs and hides for apparel and other uses. The small fauna include porcupines, beavers, muskrats, otters, grouse, squirrels, marmots, turkeys, mice, rabbits, rats, coyotes, weasels, badgers, and foxes. Here, as well as elsewhere on the Colorado Plateau, fish appear to have had little importance as a food resource.

Based upon the estimated number of rooms in the concentration of habitations on the lower north slope of Chimney Rock mesa, the primary zone of occupation, and hypothesized components of three to five individuals per family, Eddy put the population at that locality at between 624 and 1040 persons. These figures likely are too high and greatly exceed population estimates for any period in the Navajo Reservoir district. Still, some growth inevitably increased the grouping of dwellings and the size of villages. This concentration may have been a way of meeting the circumstances of a challenging environment. In efforts to feed the populace, full exploitation of the available arable land undoubtedly ensued. It was just a matter of time until the overflow had to expand onto new lands.

The Stollsteimer Valley, coming into the Piedra along the southeastern side of the Chimney Rock mesa, presumably attracted development after A.D. 1000. It was relatively broad and flat, more open to sunlight, with highly productive soil and a permanent stream. Farm plots are thought to have been cleared along the valley floor and at the mouths of ravines cut into escarpment faces on either side, but the people using the area chose not to live there. They established simple shelters for seasonal use on the ridges overlooking their fields but put their dwellings high up on the Chimney Rock cuesta. Such an upland shift among

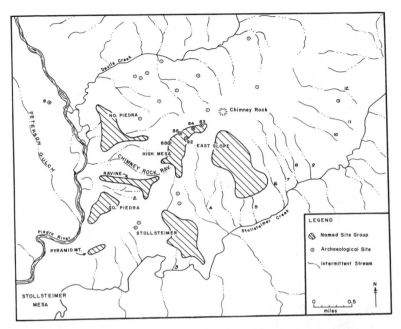

Map of seven village clusters in the Chimney Rock Archeological Area as identified by University of Colorado studies. *After Eddy, 1977, Figure 4.*

Anasazi of this time was not unusual and may hint at regionwide climatic changes, as well as the local problems of population pressures and numbing winter cold trapped in the valleys. Although the rugged terrain suggests a natural defense, there is no concrete sign that physical security was of concern other than a single possible stockade foundation across a trail and several structures strategically placed for traffic control.

The archaeological survey team counted sixteen sites scattered over the mesa wherever the broken ground permitted and crowded along the sheer northern mesa edge leading up to the multiroomed pueblo set against the backdrop of the towering stone pillars. The number of contiguous rooms at any one site was not as great as on the lower north slope. Eddy judged from surface indications that three individual houses, ten structures comprising four multiple units, and seven villages making up a total of ninety-seven rooms were represented.

Many environmental conditions were less favorable here than down below. At 7,400 feet, a slope toward the south did afford a beneficial warming exposure and longer periods of light, but among the drawbacks were more intense storms. Those in summer were accompanied by wicked lightning. There were few substantial patches of land deep enough for cultivation, and a crusty caprock complicated any sort of construction. The major problem to occupation was that there was no immediate source of water other than ephemeral seeps between the Pictured Cliff sandstone and Lewis shale.

The lack of drinking water on the high mesa tested the ingenuity of the Piedrans but was not an insurmountable problem. In winter, snow surely was melted for household use. If the mesa-top structures continued to be occupied in summer, the women and children are assumed to have carried water six hundred to a thousand feet up from the valley floors over rough trails a mile to a mile and a half long. Potters produced large plain gray jars with narrow necks and mouths in which to store this precious resource. Seepage from unglazed earthenwares resulted in considerable liquid loss. The output of such vessels in comparison to those meant for other functions was far greater here than in neighboring Anasazi outposts. Reinforcing the notion of vital storage containers filling every mesa-top home was one study of a very limited sherd lot that seemed to show that the percentage of water jars increased with distance from water sources. Because the vessels themselves were too heavy and cumbersome to carry when full and possibly wet, a different type of receptacle, perhaps tightly woven pitched baskets or skin bags, must have been employed for the actual hauling.

One can envision columns of women and offspring trudging down and up the mesa in an endless replenishment of water and groups of men hiking down to their fields in morning and back to their domiciles at night. It was not uncommon for Anasazi fields to be at some distance from settlements, but in this case the separation between home and farm was more vertical than horizontal. What to modern observers might appear as an overly arduous routine for all family members literally was taken in stride by the Anasazi, for whom life was never easy.

Despite other logistical difficulties, raw materials for building were plentiful on the mesa. The abundant cobblestones on the spurs of land

Eleventh-century small house site (5AA88) on the Chimney Rock mesa after excavation and stabilization. *Courtesy San Juan National Forest.*

next to the river were replaced at greater elevations by outcrops of sandstone. Using heavy stone mauls and hammers, workers broke out rough blocks of this material. Mud and clay for mortar and plaster were present in pockets near house sites, but water with which to prepare them either had to be collected from melting snow in spring or fall or carried up from the rivers at other seasons. A virgin forest yielded ponderosa pine and Douglas fir for primary roofing timbers and piñon and juniper for stringers and insulating layers. The Anasazi felled and prepared them with stone axes or blades, a strenuous task with which they had long experience.

The way in which the stone, earth, and wood were used to create shelters revealed both the persistence of the Piedrans' cultural biases and their adaptability to this high-altitude environment. The three multiple-unit groups excavated by the university diggers showed that the long tradition of round dwellings was ingrained in the Piedran mind-set — they continued to build them on the high mesa. It was as though a house

View of interior living room at Site 5AA88 showing its similarity to older pithouses of the upper San Juan region. *Courtesy University of Colorado.*

was not acceptable unless it was somewhat circular. Ideally, it should also be at least partially subterranean. However, with bedrock so near the surface, the masons could not sink their mesa residences any appreciable depth into the ground. They did install interior features — southern ventilator shaft, fire hearth, four post holes for seating of roof supports, and metate bins — typical of the houses to which they were accustomed. There is no remaining trace of wall plastering. In essence, the Chimney Rock mesa dwellings were pithouses without the pit.

The most unusual characteristics of these rustic edifices were massive, crudely laid masonry walls averaging three feet in thickness. In instances where several round structures were joined, the wall breadth was even greater. Doubtless this kind of wall construction was an adaptation to frigid winters on the exposed, windswept mesa top. To further maintain their customary architectural ideals, the builders attached thick-walled rectangular storage or workrooms on the north or west side of round living rooms, repeating in sandstone what earlier had been made of jacal or cobbles. This continued use into the eleventh

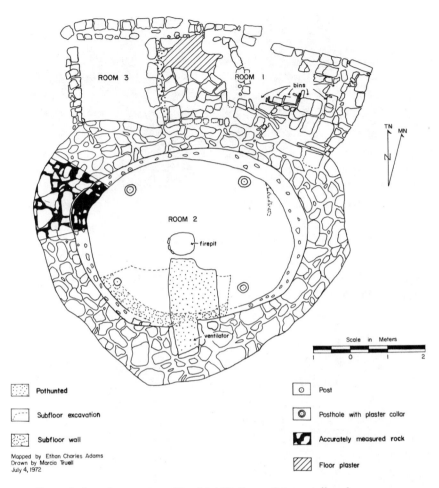

Ground plan of structure at Site 5AA88. Room 2 is partially subterranean; Rooms 1 and 3 are at ground level. *After Eddy, 1977, Figure 29.*

century of the pithouse form and its idiosyncratic appearance makes the architecture of the high-mesa Piedrans and those of contemporaries living along the far eastern peripheries of the Anasazi world distinctive from styles developed in either the Chaco or Mesa Verde areas.

The eleventh-century Piedrans not only favored pithouses, they also had a penchant for putting them on high places. For example, surveyors found two settlements on a sharp pinnacle called Pyramid Mountain, an

A line of milling bins in Room 1 at Site 5AA88 indicates that space was a work area. *Courtesy San Juan National Forest.*

A cache of grinding stones and mauls was recovered in a special-function surface room at Site 5AA88. *Courtesy University of Colorado.*

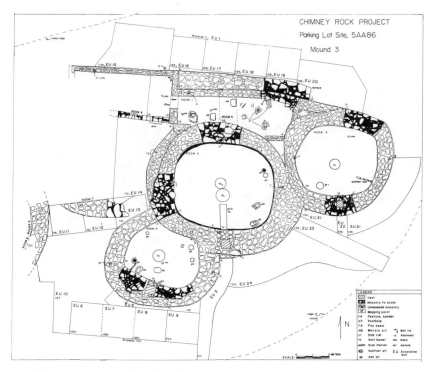

Plan of the Parking Lot Site (5AA86) showing three partially subterranean living rooms flanked on the north by several surface workrooms. *After Eddy, 1977, Figure 25.*

erosional remnant that rises some 250 feet above the southwestern rim of the Chimney Rock mesa. The sides of the peak are steeply sloped, difficult to negotiate, and impossible to cultivate. The area on top of it is so limited and spiny that twelve mounds and pithouse depressions are crammed together as if hanging on. The summit commands an awe-inspiring 360-degree view of the merger of river valleys six hundred feet below with successive tiers of evergreen mountains. Nonetheless, there seems no practical reason to have selected this spot for home sites. Thus, some students regard the Pyramid Mountain group of sites as a ceremonial center, an idea for which there is as yet no supporting evidence.

One excavated structure on Chimney Rock mesa does appear to have served some special function. It was probably both ritualistic and

Parking Lot Site after excavation and stabilization. *Courtesy San Juan National Forest*.

secular in nature and helped to integrate the scattered mesa-top occupants into a viable social unit. Eddy called it a "Great Kiva." However, morphologically its relationship to other eastern Anasazi Great Kivas was more that of a second cousin than of a twin. Rather than being substantially below ground level, the Chimney Rock structure was primarily a surficial chamber built on bedrock that sloped southward. Rather than being a true circle in shape, it had a slightly convoluted exterior wall. Rather than having wall niches or encircling rooms for special objects, it featured fourteen rectangular cists sunk into the perimeter of the floor. Rather than being equipped with a bench around the entire circumference, it sported a narrow, finlike projection on the north side of the room that would have served only as a shelf and not as seating for spectators of events going on in the chamber. According to custom, a pair of crudely laid masonry floor vaults was placed on a north-south axis on opposite sides of the kiva. They were irregular in shape but nonetheless vaguely rectangular, as were those known in other districts. Although more semicircular than square, the surviving foundation of a central masonry box suggests the usual fireboxes in other

Excavator Frank Eddy stands on a photography ladder at the Parking Lot Site while a helicopter overhead delivers stabilization materials. *Courtesy University of Colorado.*

Great Kivas. Because the stones were not fire-reddened, Eddy preferred to regard the feature as an altar. However, that term ascribes a religious purpose to something others see as strictly utilitarian.

Whether or not the building was roofed is another open question. Little evidence of fallen wooden roof members and just one of the typical four spaced post holes for vertical supports were found. It is possible that the timbers may have been removed at some time for other use. Further, three posts may have rested on bedrock, eliminating the need for seating holes. Although an estimated wall height of less than four feet strength-

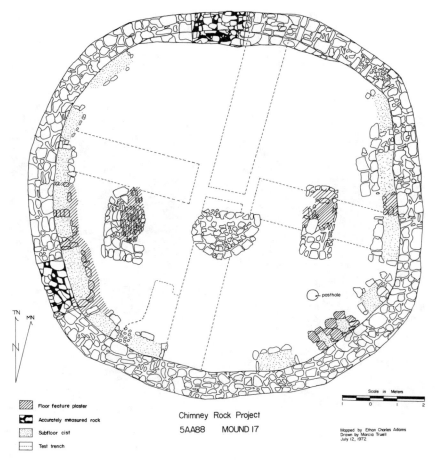

▨	Floor feature plaster
◧	Accurately measured rock
▦	Subfloor cist
┈	Test trench

Chimney Rock Project

5AA88   MOUND 17

Scale in Meters

Mapped by Ethan Charles Adams
Drawn by Marcia Truell
July 12, 1972

Plan of Chimney Rock Great Kiva (Site 5AA88, Mound 17). *After Eddy, 1977, Figure 28.*

ens the no-roof hypothesis, it was obvious to the excavators that much of the superstructure had been removed prehistorically. In view of the prevailing lack of architectural refinement seen in the Piedran structures, it might well have been beyond the builders' capabilities to span the more than forty-foot diameter of this structure. A partial roof was an alternative. However, an exposed chamber collecting snow from October to June and filling with rainwater in summer could have been of little use. Contributing to the mystery of this building is the matter

Great Kiva after 1971–1972 excavation. Note roots of large trees that had grown over the wall of the abandoned structure. *Courtesy University of Colorado.*

Great Kiva on Chimney Rock mesa after stabilization. One floor vault is at right. Rocks in the center may have been a collapsed firebox. A partial narrow bench runs along the north wall; opened floor pits are at right. A small house (Site 5AA88) is visible at center rear. *Courtesy San Juan National Forest.*

of how it was entered. The usual surface antechamber and stairs leading down into a subsurface room were absent, suggesting either that there was no roof or that there was a roof hatchway. Although an awkward way to get into such a large surface building, to Piedrans accustomed to hatchway entrances to their above-ground pithouses it would have seemed a logical solution. Was the whole structure a botched job, or were the Piedrans simply doing their own thing?

The portable artifacts taken from the structure were the usual stone implements — axes, choppers, and gravers. Fragments of plain gray earthenware jars were present. No ceremonial goods were found, but that does not necessarily indicate a strictly social usage of the building. Four small rectangular earthenware blocks with holes, in which it has been suggested feathers could be inserted, were found in the nearby dwelling and may have been part of ritual accoutrements used in the large chamber. Some relationship between the two neighboring buildings is possible.

Tree-ring analysis of wood specimens from the multiroomed domestic structure indicates that trees needed for construction were cut during summer months. Generally, Anasazi farmers at lower elevations reserved this activity for periods of the year when crops did not need tending. Eddy suggests a time of plentiful rainfall that allowed farmers the freedom to do other tasks. Planks for the kiva floor cists were cut from summer-harvested wood. The range of tree-ring dates for the cist planks is from A.D. 994 to 1084. The early date likely came from a piece of old downed wood that was picked up and put to use. The latter may have come from a replacement for a worn specimen. Of twelve dates, one-third were in the 1070s. That period seems a probable construction time for the large building. Although there was an earlier occupation at the nearby house, the 1070s also represented an active building episode there.

With this one obviously specialized structure verified through excavation, it is possible that other large depressions on the lower terraces, some up to seventy feet in diameter, contain similar remains. From Piedra Phase times, villages on the San Juan usually included one oversized pithouse that most regional archaeologists interpret as a community center. The concept of such a building likely was carried up the Piedra. However, the number of large depressions in the environs of

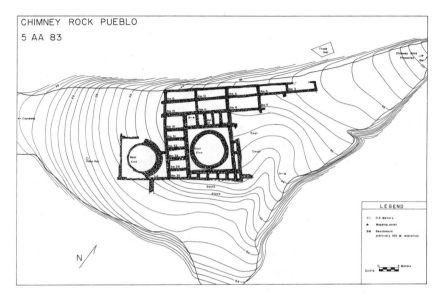

Plan of the excavated portions of the Chimney Rock pueblo (Site 5AA83). *After Eddy, 1977, Figure 12.*

Chimney Rock (Eddy cites thirty-six) is too great for the normal ratio of Great Kivas to domiciles. Could it be that the insularity of the upper Piedrans gave rise to a religious intensification requiring more special places in which to perform rituals? Recovered materials do not reflect such an elaboration. Nor are there small kivas for more intimate cere-monies such as typify other Anasazi villages.

As the eleventh century drew to a close and after long periods of virtual isolation from the rest of the Anasazi world, a thunderbolt of outside influence hit the Chimney Rock mesa. This influence was expressed in the large pueblo on the caprock of the most prominent 7,600-foot level of the cuesta, from where it dominated the lower indigenous settlements. Jeancon's judgment in 1921 that it was reflec-tive of the architectural style of Chaco Canyon was reaffirmed in 1970, when the university crew removed fallen debris and carried out limited excavation. What was exposed was the ruin of an edificial form known in Chaco studies as a Great House. It was a planned, multistory room-block of core and veneer sandstone masonry, with large, high-ceilinged rooms and incorporated dual kivas, one of which was of a Chacoan style. It was totally unlike any other architectural complex on the Piedra.

At the time of Jeancon's work, the Chimney Rock pueblo was only the second such Chacoan structure excavated outside Chaco Canyon itself. The first was at Aztec Ruins in New Mexico forty miles southwest of Chimney Rock. The relationships of these sites to broader Chaco regional developments were not explored at the time the remains were originally studied. Only after another half-century of research would it be realized that these two sites were part of a network of similar structures that stretched out in all directions from the hub of Chaco Canyon, in some cases as far as several hundred miles. Now known as "outliers," these structures are regarded as manifestations of a burst of efflorescence. During a period of about seventy-five years straddling the eleventh and twelfth centuries, Anasazi culture in bleak, resource-deficient Chaco Canyon came to an amazing climax called the Chaco Phenomenon. The number of identified Great Houses is now in excess of seventy-five, with more being found yearly. Not only were the edifices built according to a more-or-less standardized model, but the entire outlier system was organized. Commonly, Great Houses were built within a dense settlement, situated on a prominence, spaced approximately seventeen miles apart, and occasionally in late times positioned on a roadway. Frequently, a Great Kiva was also in the locality. The relationship of all these Great Houses to each other remains unknown.

The Chimney Rock Great House varied from this format. It stood at one side of the indigenous high mesa community, removed from the aggregates of dwellings rather than in the center of occupation. Topography probably dictated this placement. As indicated, the large, specialized chamber farther down the mesa top does not fit the Great Kiva stereotype and seems to date from as much as fifteen to twenty years earlier. As yet, no Great House has been documented in the intervening region between Chimney Rock and its nearest Chacoan neighbor, Aztec Ruins, making the distance between them more than twice the usual amount for outliers. Nor has a prehistoric road been noted in the vicinity. Roberts's chance discovery closer to the San Juan of a small basin cut into bedrock and a possible signaling station, both features commonly associated with the Chacoan sphere, lead one to suspect that somewhere

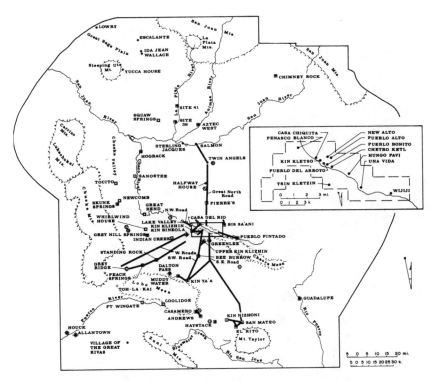

Known system of prehistoric Chaco roads does not reach as far north as Chimney Rock. *After Powers, Gillespie, and Lekson, 1983, Figure 1.*

in the unexplored lands south of Chimney Rock another Great House eventually may be found.

Aside from preparing the way for public visitation at the Chimney Rock Great House, the university researchers sought wood samples from which to obtain the dates that Jeancon was unable to provide. They were successful in this effort but prompted a controversy that remains unresolved. One cross pole from the ventilator shaft of the lower east kiva produced a tree-ring date of A.D. 1076. Eddy accepts that date as the time of the building of the kiva and, by extension, the remainder of the roomblock. However, colleagues suspect that the wood specimen probably was a reused timber salvaged from one of the structures on the lower mesa. Supporting this idea is the fact that of fifty-three dates

Archaeologists wrapping tree-ring specimens from Room 8 of the Chimney Rock pueblo, some of which yielded a probable cutting date of A.D. 1093. *Courtesy University of Colorado.*

obtained from wood samples recovered in the local small sites, twenty-six are in the 1070s, whereas only two of the forty-seven specimens reclaimed from the Great House are of that decade. Consequently, these researchers believe the Great House construction was accomplished in one short-term effort in the 1090s. Twenty-six samples of the fallen ceiling wood from one room securely date to 1093, and five eroded samples from the rebuilt east kiva also likely were cut in that year. Eddy proposes that a second remodeling of the site took place then to repair or change what was done in 1076. However, the east kiva and other sectors of the houseblock actually could have been redone while general construction was still underway, perhaps to correct miscalculations in planning, rather than seventeen years after initial construction.

If this revised dating interpretation is correct, the Great House erection postdated known construction in the indigenous community by a decade and a half or more. The most recent date from the local structures is the 1084 Great Kiva cist plank, which may not reflect time of building. That is not to say that the local populace was gone. A partially burned branch taken from a domestic firepit in an indigenous house dates to 1087, and proposed dates for pollen from the fill of another hearth range from 1090 to 1100. The 1090s also witnessed intense building efforts within Chaco Canyon, as well as outlier construction elsewhere north of the San Juan River, including that at the Salmon and Lowry ruins.

The enigma of the Chimney Rock Great House begins with the identity of its builders. Its style and the degree of craftsmanship exhibited in most of its construction suggest that a cadre of Chaco masons migrated northward to do the job. Were they conquerors, colonists, or neither? There is no indication that the intrusion was accompanied by force. If they were colonists, traders, or missionaries, how did they communicate with the local people? Some linguists now think the Chacoans spoke Keresan and the Piedrans spoke Tewa. Others believe all people in the northern San Juan spoke Tewa. The best farm plots surely had been worked for generations by the Piedrans; did the Chacoans, because they had more power or more experience with water control and other agricultural methods, simply take these plots? Or did they impose some sort of tribute in the form of goods or foodstuffs? Did they regard the Piedrans as country bumpkins who were not even able to build a proper Great Kiva? Provocative as these questions are, it is improbable that the outliers were the product of companies of male colonists who permanently left their womenfolk at home. One theory, noting the large number of outliers and the number of them being erected at the same time, has specialized construction crews being dispatched from Chaco Canyon to carry out the various building projects. This work may have been done in return for services or products from the local populace. It is also possible that the Chaco influence was so pervasive across the entire eastern Colorado Plateau by the close of the eleventh century that local workers became willing apprentices under the guidance of a Chacoan *mayordomo*. The fact that the western portion of the houseblock was less well constructed and the associated kiva lacked usual Chacoan characteristics may reflect indigenous workmanship.

A diluted Chaco style of masonry was noted by Roberts in 1922 in one small house the State Historical and Natural History Society crew dug on a lower terrace. Some pottery and bits of turquoise taken from its fill dirt likewise pointed to a Chaco connection. This site, and perhaps others as yet unexcavated, could have resulted either from a direct intrusion of Chacoans or, more likely, some locals strongly under the Chaco spell.

Regardless of who was responsible for building the Chimney Rock Great House, the task was a formidable one. Just what was the motivating force behind its presence in a backward community with little prior association with Chacoans and on a piece of property that seemingly presented no practical advantage? The selection of that location and the sheer difficulty of building there can be seen as symbolizing authority, which leads to the explanation for the outlier system. Many scholars now believe that it was devised and administered by a Chacoan elite as a means of bringing a continual supply of required resources into the core area of Chaco Canyon or redistributing them to satellites in return for some sort of sociopolitical, economic, or religious patronage, if not actual goods. The primary resource the upper Piedra district could have provided under such a scheme was timber used in Chaco Canyon, where there were almost no trees yet where hundreds of thousands of logs were utilized. The Chimney Rock cuesta may have been especially attractive because ponderosa pines were available on the lower slopes. Archaeologist Allan Kane would have the men controlling this traffic living in the Chimney Rock Great House, postulating the simpler structures down the mesa as the lumberjacks' camps and those on the bluffs nearer the river as the point at which crews actually floated logs downriver to some point such as Salmon Ruin, from where they could have been transported via a road into Chaco. This is a fascinating but as yet unverifiable plot. Studies of trace elements in wood recovered at Chaco eventually may pin down a number of sources, the slopes of the Chuskas to the west of Chaco among them. The low frequency in the Chimney Rock assemblages of stone tools that could have been used in logging discounts the notion of such specialized activity. Also, even though some timber may well have been taken from the Chimney Rock district, why put the command post on top of a thousand-foot-high mesa, where there was nothing more than a view? How were simple farmers, whose preceding dozen generations had laboriously tilled the terraces, converted into virtual chain gangs of wholesale woodsmen? Would they have accepted such interference with their traditional round of summer duties? And what did the locals get in return? Apparently not material things: virtually nothing came from the excavators' trenches that could be identified as diagnostically Chacoan other than a handful of potsherds and several tiny flakes of turquoise. The lack of classic Chaco pottery can be explained in part by its very restricted distribution away from the canyon proper and the wholesale switch in the early twelfth century across the northern San Juan Basin to a vegetal-painted McElmo style.

What some scholars believe the Piedrans did get from an inflow of Chaco power was a recharging of religious batteries. One school of thought has the Great House edging up to the feet of the sacred stony Twin War Gods in order to bask in their aura and draw strength or protection. For some 250 years the Piedrans lived with these anthropomorphized pillars on the eastern horizon, and, if present custom gives any indication, felt their supernatural energy and perhaps appeased them with offerings or prayers. Why at the end of the eleventh century should they feel compelled to move closer? Maybe because of some Chacoan drive toward greater concern for help from their gods.

Another school argues that the houseblock was built as a watchtower from which to observe astronomical phenomena having great importance in regulating the ceremonial calendar, which in turn was bound up with the yearly cycle of planting and harvesting. An accurate calendar would have been of utmost importance to a group in a marginal agricultural setting, where a few weeks too early or too late in planting could have been disastrous for crops. Although most identified celestial features among Anasazi remains have to do with the sun, from whom the Twin War Gods descended, astronomer McKim Malville points out a sequence of lunar events that might have been watched during the second half of the eleventh century by Chimney Rock residents. The moon has symbolic life and death meaning for the Pueblo Indians of today, and its monthly cycle segments the year. Malville's computer-determined phenomena include full moons rising between the pinnacles near the time of three winter solstices, a particularly significant time for modern Pueblo Indians, or another three periods called lunar standstills, when the moon has reached sufficiently high northern declination to appear between the columns as many as forty times per period. Malville ties these lunar events to the two tree-ring dates of 1076 and 1093 obtained from the Great House. He suggests that observations around 1076 prompted refurbishing of the Great House at the later date in order to create a more adequate viewing place. However, he fails to note that there is no information available about the exact form of the upper walls of the edifice or whether they would have improved viewing opportunities.

Over the years, the Piedrans were on hand to take note of the standstill periods, fourteen or fifteen of which occurred before June 1094, and the more frequent correspondence of full moon and winter solstices. Even though the view from the lower mesa might have been obscured because of the lay of the land or less dramatic than the view from higher up, and even though it would not have had the pinnacles as an immediate foresight, quite surely the Piedrans observed these celestial dramas with keen interest. Moreover, Malville's team determined that an indigenous house structure on the highlands west of the Piedra River and a supposed tower on the Chimney Rock mesa were in the necessary alignment with the two chimneys to serve as places from which sun watchers could have made calculations relative to the solar solstices. The alleged tower happened to be situated in the side of a swale that might have hampered observations, and its upper construction is unknown. Whether or not such site locations were coincidental will never be known for sure. But would prior interest in sunrises silhouetting the stone columns and moonrises shining through the space between them have prompted the Piedrans to help the Chacoans raise the large building crowning the mesa? Perhaps yes, if they were overwhelmed by a desire to share in whatever magic it was that the Chacoans briefly exerted over their fellow eastern Anasazi. In Malville's view, the Cha-

Small, solid clay slabs punctured with spaced holes may have been holders for sacred feather plumes. In addition to eleven specimens reclaimed from Chimney Rock settlements, others have been found in prehistoric remains in Chaco Canyon and appear to have been used in modern times in Hopi ceremonies. *Courtesy Marcia Truell Newren.*

coans were so astronomically sophisticated they would have exploited for their own ends a local knowledge of these lunar phenomena. To him, the guardhouse, the tiny building spanning the narrow ridge of land leading up to the Great House (excavated for a third time in 1988), was meant to control traffic into a sacred precinct dedicated to astronomical purposes. If that were in fact the reason for the Chimney Rock Great House, it would be the only outlier thus far linked specifically to religion.

The Chimney Rock Great House itself was not any sort of specialized ceremonial edifice, nor did it need architects trained in skills restricted to a religious elite that may or may not have been attuned to what was taking place in the sky. Albeit of more refined construction than most, in many respects the Great House was just like scores of other roomblocks found from southwestern Colorado to the Little Colorado drainage of west central New Mexico and eastern Arizona. It may have been meant as nonresidential public architecture, even though it was partly occupied: if the motivation for its establishment was ritualistic in nature, it may have been a center to which periodic pilgrimages were directed. However, there is no known road along which the faithful may have traveled nor is there sufficient residue of material things to confirm large-scale gatherings or feasting.

The one category of goods recovered that might conceivably be interpreted as ceremonial are eleven so-called feather holders, only several of which were found in the large pueblo. One came from the fill of the east kiva. Technical analyses of the clays from which they were formed indicate five different unidentified sources. Perhaps feather holders made at a number of places were carried to Chimney Rock for special rites. Several have been found in Chaco.

Whatever the reasons for putting the Chimney Rock Great House where it is, the adventure was short-lived. After only two further lunar standstills and the cutting of several thousand logs, it was all over. Beginning about A.D. 1130–1135, the great design evolved at Chaco Canyon started to collapse, taking many of the outliers, probably including that at Chimney Rock, with it. In the wake of failure, neither astronomical observations nor procurement of resources was important. Some outliers were reoccupied by Mesa Verdeans after the twelfth-century Chaco abandonment, but Chimney Rock was not among them.

Another of the many unanswered questions concerning Chimney Rock is whether the Piedrans themselves may have led the exodus from the area. If so, the absence of a local support group could have hastened the demise of the outlier as a cog in the Chaco system. Conversely, without the presumed unifying force of the Chaco Phenomenon, the indigenous population may have been more vulnerable to debilitating circumstances. One of these was another dry cycle that gripped the upper San Juan district as the Great House construction began. It eased for a time early in the twelfth century, only to become very severe after 1130. If they had not already departed, that prolonged drought surely would have prompted the Piedra Anasazi to move on. After they left, the

Chimney Rock district would never again be home to as many individuals as it had been during their tenure.

When the Piedrans did leave the mesa, it was not just a matter of their going to another terrace several miles upriver. This time they moved off the Colorado Plateau. Did they look back and ponder the trauma of leaving the Twin War Gods? Or if they took comfort in the presence of these deities, did they feel betrayed when things turned sour?

A route proposed by scholars would have taken the Piedrans south along the San Juan River to where Largo and Gobernador canyons opened to the east. As the migrants went up these pathways toward the Continental Divide, they were among peoples sharing a similar cultural base. A familiar variety of architecture and settlement patterns and a comparable array of portable material things eased their way. By the end of the twelfth century, the Piedrans are thought to have reached the Gallina uplands in New Mexico, northwest of modern Jemez Pueblo. It was an environment in which they were comfortable, one of high mesas dissected by canyons in a transition zone between ponderosa pine and juniper. Architectural and artifactual evidence confirms that they settled there for about another century, after which they disappeared from the cultural record.

Several elders of Taos Pueblo, the northernmost of the modern Pueblo Indian villages, claim that one of their clans originated at the Chimney Rock communities. To date, there is no archaeological confirmation of this legend in any direct line between the two localities. The long passage covering several centuries from the foot of the San Juan Mountains to the foot of the Sangre de Cristo Mountains may have looped southward through the Gallina district.

Back at Chimney Rock, the empty houses fell into ruin. Many roofs burned. Perhaps they were ignited by departing occupants. Perhaps lightning struck them or nearby trees, setting them ablaze. The charred or rotted timbers sank inward into the above-ground pithouses, leaving the landscape scarred with man-made craters. The great paired pinnacles topping the cuesta were enveloped in a deep silence that remained unbroken for nearly half a millennium.

PART III

EPILOGUE

5

THE CHIMNEY ROCK DISTRICT
TO 1900

In the fall of 1626 a group of Capote Utes walked several hundred miles out of their customary hunting grounds in the San Juan Mountains to Jemez. They established a camp close by. On this occasion their purpose was to trade hides, dried meat, and berries for salt, textiles, and foodstuffs raised by the Pueblo Indian farmers. In other winters their southerly migrations to the vicinity of the northwesternmost Spanish settlement of Abiquiu typically were to escape from severe cold. When spring arrived at Jemez, the Capotes again packed up and traveled back along the Chama River to the foot of the craggy mountains and then northwest into the recesses of what is now southern Colorado. They very likely paused for a time to enjoy the waters of a large, bubbling thermal spring at a bend in the San Juan River just twenty miles east of Chimney Rock and Companion Rock. Periodic long-term interactions such as this one between the nomadic mountain tribes and the sedentary villagers of the Rio Grande probably was an established pattern, but in 1626 it was noted by Spanish scribes at Santa Fe for the first time. The Capote Utes had come out from the shadows of the rocks and briefly entered documented history, only to soon disappear back into their lofty wilderness.

Three of the seven distinct bands of Utes occupied a large swath of land along the northern flanks of the Spanish holdings in New Mexico. The Capotes claimed the territory from the headwaters of the San Juan River west to the upper Animas River, including a huge slice of the mountains buttressing the north side of this region. On further west toward what is now the Four Corners were the Wiminuches. East of the

Capotes in the San Luis Valley and along the eastern slopes of the Rockies and bordering plains were the Moaches.

Exactly where and when the Utes originated as a tribe remains unclear. Being constantly on the move in search of game and edible plants and having only meager worldly goods, they left little imprint upon the land for archaeologists to study. It is generally believed, however, that sometime between the fifteenth and sixteenth centuries they drifted down through the great western intermontane basin, gradually spreading through 150,000 square miles of semiarid eastern Utah, western Colorado, and into the Rocky Mountains. The fact that they spoke a Shoshonean language similar to that of the Hopis of north central Arizona, the Paiutes of southern Utah, and the Comanches of the southern plains suggests a remote common ancestry.

Prehistoric Ute occupation in this vast area has been noted by the occasional residue of brush huts, game traps, rock art, and a few small objects used in food gathering and processing. The latter include chipped projectile points, stone choppers, handstones, and milling slabs, tatters of baskets or cordage, and rare, poorly made earthenware jars. Generally speaking, the Utes shared an impoverished Desert Culture that had been typical of other Great Basin groups for several thousand years. That is what they likely carried as cultural attributes whenever they arrived in the Chimney Rock district.

But then a fundamental change took place because the temptation to own Spanish horses proved irresistible. By the 1640s the Southern Utes were the first western tribe to be mounted after stealing or trading for animals from neighboring Spanish *rancherías* and pastures. Learning to skillfully handle and breed the stock changed their character. No longer were they shy primitives hiding behind the peaks. Emboldened with new self-confidence, they traveled far and wide. This mobility brought them for the first time into significant association with surrounding Native Americans and with Europeans. Both offered advantages and posed threats.

The Southern Utes seem to have been most influenced by their linguistic relatives, the Comanches. Because the Moaches were geographically closest to these people, they served as agents in introducing some aspects of borrowed Plains culture to other Utes. Leather leggings and untailored outer garments were adopted. Interest in quill-, feather-, and beadwork grew accordingly. Skin-covered tepees replaced the brush wickiups erected earlier. Although the Comanches and the Moache Utes enjoyed a friendly alliance during the years when both were becoming increasingly aggressive and wide-ranging and both relied at times on help from the Jicarilla Apaches, the relationships eventually broke down, with repeated casualties on all sides.

Throughout the seventeenth century there were conflicts between Spaniards and Utes. The primary band involved appears to have been the Moaches, whose range overlapped that of the northern probings of the Spanish realm. Territorial rights were at stake. The Capotes remained secure in a region still unexplored by Europeans but periodically came into Spanish communities to trade hides, buffalo robes, and slaves for metal tools, beads, and the fine blankets made by the Pueblos. Such intercourse hastened an acculturation that was slow in coming to the Capotes because of their remoteness. In 1670 the Spaniards signed a treaty with the Southern Ute bands, and none are thought to have joined the revolt spearheaded by the Pueblos that ten years later drove the hated white masters out of New Mexico for a twelve-year period.

That uprising did directly affect the Capotes, however. At the end of the seventeenth century some Navajos and residents of Jemez banded together to move into Capote territory in order to escape probable Spanish reprisals against them. At the time, the San Juan River was considered a natural, if highly permeable, border between Navajos and Capote and Wiminuche Utes. One of the earliest Spanish explorers into the district recognized this fact when he noted, "This stream [San Juan River] is called the Rio Grande del Navajo because it separates the province of this name from the Yuta nation" (Motter 1984, 25).

Prehistorically, Navajos in some number lived along most of the northern tributaries of the San Juan, although many more concentrated in the broken tablelands drained by the Largo and Gobernador rivers to the south. That was the homeland they now know as the Dinetah. Whether the Piedra River valley was one of those utilized by Navajos prior to 1700 remains a question for future research. If so, it is possible that incoming Utes routed them out for a time.

As with the Utes, nothing about the Navajos or their cultural heritage prior to their appearance in the Southwest is known. The point of origination of Athabaskan-speaking Apachean bands, which include the Navajos, is suggested to have been in the Mackenzie Basin of Canada. In the course of many centuries, they made their way south, reaching the northern Colorado Plateau some time after the departure of the Anasazi and before the arrival of the Utes along the region's northern perimeters. Recent archaeology puts them in the La Plata drainage of southwestern Colorado by the mid-1400s. The first Spanish reference to the Navajos places them in the greater Southwest at the time of Coronado's 1540 *entrada*. Early Navajo social or ceremonial organization is unstudied, but this group differed from its Apache relatives in engaging in rudimentary farming to supplement a basic hunting and gathering subsistence. That lifestyle required seasonal sedentism, which is substantiated by occasional finds of remains of their shelters. These were created by upright logs arranged in a tight circle and interlocked at their tops to form a conical frame, and the whole was made secure by a covering of earth, brush, and stones. A rough utilitarian kind of pottery, quite distinctive from that made by the Pueblos, is found associated with these structures. Also recovered are simple stone implements used in hunting and in food preparation.

The mixed group of peoples who took refuge in Capote territory following the Spanish reconquest of New Mexico in 1692 appears to have preferred the more open valleys to the west of the Piedra, which afforded better horticultural possibilities. However, this impression may result from lack of archaeology along the central section of the Piedra rather than absence of relevant sites there. A limited refugee occupation did occur at the now submerged confluence of the San Juan and Piedra rivers, and a scattering of seventeenth-century Pueblo potsherds has been recorded within sight of the Chimney Rock–Companion Rock pinnacles.

There is not as much evidence north of the San Juan of the cultural transfusion that occurred elsewhere, wherein Navajo culture was revamped according to the Pueblo model. Nor is there the assortment of Spanish goods — bullet casings, metal axes and hammers, pieces of glazed earthenware, sheep bones — that might have come into Navajo

Remains of an eighteenth-century Navajo forked-stick hogan in the Navajo Reservoir district (Site LA 4071). *Courtesy Museum of New Mexico.*

hands through the Pueblos. This absence of evidence reflects the fact that the refugee influx north of the San Juan was an overflow from the Dinetah and probably involved only a few hundred Navajos and a handful of Pueblos who were geographically separated from the central zone of contact. The upper San Juan was a cultural backwater then as it had been when the Anasazi were around. Its most obvious remains of the refugee period are the usual Navajo forked-stick hogans, *ramadas*, fire hearths, storage pits, and camps in rock overhangs. Only infrequently are these structures situated near the small cellular masonry rooms in defensive locations believed to have been used by the Pueblo contingent. Any significant impact on Navajo house style by the Pueblos is lacking. However, rock art scratched or painted on cliff faces suggests a notable elaboration of Navajo costume and ritual attributable to Pueblo influence. Pottery of typical tapered-bottom Navajo forms but bearing painted decoration; holes in houses' dirt floors to support looms; clay spindle whorls; wooden prayer sticks and bull roarers; stone bird fetishes; and other lesser objects are further indications of an upgrading

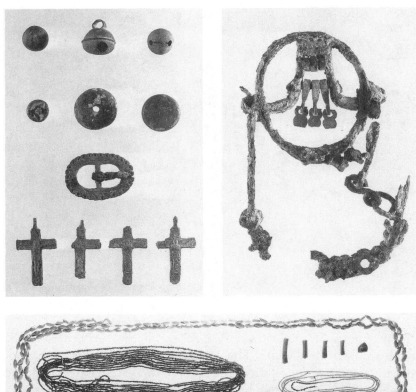

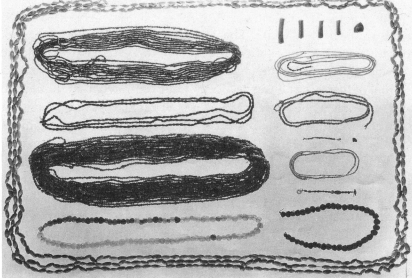

Metal crosses bearing figures of the Savior and the Virgin, metal buttons, buckle, horse gear, and many feet of variously colored glass beads were left behind in structures south of the San Juan River occupied by Pueblo Indians fleeing Spanish reprisals after the revolt of 1680–1692. *Courtesy University of Colorado Museum, Earl Morris Collection.*

Early eighteenth-century Pueblo refugee structure on the Gobernador drainage of New Mexico south of the San Juan River. *Courtesy University of Colorado Museum, Earl Morris Collection.*

of Navajo culture as a result of the years of cohabitation. Moreover, Pueblo influence flowed to the Navajos from the distant past. These early Navajos may not yet have acquired an ingrained fear of the spirits of the dead — they rifled some of the many ancient Pueblo antiquities to be found along the main and side channels of the upper San Juan, reclaiming stone and bone implements that had been discarded hundreds of years earlier. They also converted Anasazi burial chambers into storage places.

The Capotes tolerated the intruders for about fifty years. At the end of that time, the small Pueblo population either had been absorbed by the larger Navajo community or had returned to its traditional home. At mid-eighteenth century, resentful over unwanted competition for resources, the Utes rose up and drove the Navajos back south of the San Juan River. For the next hundred years the Capotes continued to regard the Navajos as their enemies. On occasion they went as far south as

Mount Taylor or southwest to Canyon de Chelly to attack the Navajos on their own ground. This enmity eventually peaked in the 1860s when U.S. troops employed Ute scouts to track down Navajos for incarceration at Fort Sumner.

The aggression against Navajos was just one expression of warlike attitudes on the part of the Capotes. As strong, mounted nomads worldwide have done, they took advantage of more peaceful, earthbound farmers. During the late seventeenth and throughout the eighteenth century, the Capotes preyed upon the sedentary agricultural Hopis, swooping out of their mountain fastness and riding pell-mell across the barren wastes of the San Juan Basin, lured westward by granaries full of corn and beans. Then they turned on the Spaniards of the lower Chama River valley. The Utes left the unprotected mud villages of Abiquiu, Ojo Caliente, and Embudo in ruins. By 1747 Spanish authorities had endured enough. They launched a counteroffensive, only to learn firsthand that the Capotes had an advantage: a haven hostile to unknowledgeable outsiders.

For the 150 years that New Mexico had been a province of the Spanish Crown, the area beyond the high mountains ringing the western San Luis Valley of southern Colorado, the hunting grounds of the Capotes, remained unknown to Europeans. The first non-Indian party believed to have penetrated this pristine domain was that of Juan María Rivera, who in 1765 crossed into the San Juan Mountains and lived to tell of his travels. Eleven years later friars Domínguez and Escalante, on their unsuccessful journey to map a route from Santa Fe to San Francisco, worked down along the terraces hemming in the San Juan River. One of its northern tributaries they knew as the *Río de la Piedra Parada*, named for a pair of towering stone columns seen far away against the skyline of this drainage. Whether they or an earlier unidentified party actually first applied this name is uncertain. Eager to move westward, Domínguez and Escalante did not venture up the stream but were the first to make written mention of its dominating natural monuments. None of these initial *entradas* had any significant effect upon the natives of the district.

Once it was shown to be possible to go and come safely through this uncharted world of extreme topography and unknown numbers of Ute savages, an adventurous few Spaniards back on the Rio Grande were eager to establish trade relations with the Indians. In earlier times it was the Utes themselves who had initiated an active exchange of supple deer and elk hides processed by Capote women for desired woolen goods, beads, and utensils. Winter after winter as they pitched their tepees in the Chama Valley bottom below Abiquiu, some of the band went further downriver to trade with residents of San Juan and Santa Clara pueblos or to walk the streets of Santa Fe quietly waiting for Spanish customers. However, in the late eighteenth century, in order to promote a greater volume of exchange, the Spanish colonial government began licensing individuals to take their commodities directly to nomadic Indians circling the fringes of European civilization. Some unscrupulous men hastened to exploit this opening and dealt in contraband whiskey and guns. Whether legitimate or not, this frontier commerce yielded an important benefit to the administration: a growing knowledge of the northwestern outlands.

As the Mexican administration took over New Mexico in the early 1800s, the Chimney Rock district of southern Colorado was rapidly being opened up. A number of trails used by itinerant traders out of the Rio Grande Valley already snaked through what had been virgin Capote range. Paths along the watercourses were tramped down by a rag-tag assemblage of beaver trappers, horse thieves, fur traders, and mountain men headquartered at Taos. English names dotting contemporary accounts indicate they were largely from the United States. In 1829 a 1,200-mile-long mule track, grandly termed the Old Spanish Trail (although the Spaniards never had traversed it), was blazed from Santa Fe to Los Angeles. Its first sectors followed a Capote route from Abiquiu north up the Chama River, across some of the highlands where Navajo and Pueblo refugees once had hidden, then across the San Juan River at its junction with the Piedra, before taking off for the arid mesa country of Utah. It was in active use during the 1830s and 1840s by muleteers driving annual caravans laden with bundles of Pueblo blankets from New Mexico to California and returning with strings of hundreds of horses and mules. The Capotes, many then camped along the lower Piedra under the leadership of a man named Tamuche, resigned themselves to the movement of this foreign traffic through their southern territory. Meanwhile, Mexican settlers, who posed a more enduring threat, were closing in. The broad San Luis Valley north of Taos attracted some; Moache warriors burned them out. North of Abiquiu, the Tierra Amarilla land grant finalized in 1832 brought Hispanos to the verdant foothills of the San Juan Mountains, which the Capotes regarded as theirs. Despite their reputation for settling scores without much provocation, the Capotes observed an amazing few years of peace in the upper San Juan–Chama region. With the United States standing at the gates, that was soon to change.

The decade of the 1850s was a time of travail for all Native Americans in the northern Southwest, even more so for the newly installed U.S. territorial government. It had to maintain order across a piece of the continent it scarcely knew, populated with peoples of many backgrounds it did not understand. One of the first moves it made was to secure a treaty with Capote and Moache elders. Their hungry followers had taken to raiding Mexican farms of the upper Chama area because of threatened starvation. Hunting activities by Hispanos and other whites encroaching upon tribal lands had decimated or driven away much of the wildlife upon which the Indians depended. Kit Carson, newly appointed U.S. Indian agent, estimated that there were then between eight and nine thousand Capotes. Under treaty terms, he was responsible for issuing them rations out of a hastily established depot set up at Abiquiu. Soon a second treaty was negotiated, with stipulations that in return for dole the Capotes would try farming. To agriculturally oriented Americans, that seemed the surest alternative to depending for survival upon the providence of an uncontrolled nature. To the Utes, whose hunting and gathering tradition was millennia long, it was unthinkable. Dole continued; farming never commenced.

U.S. penetration into the heart of Capote territory began in 1859, when an army party headed by Capt. John N. Macomb of the Corps of Topographical Engineers set out to retrace the Old Spanish Trail into Utah. The men went from Abiquiu, the jumping-off place for northern explorations, to the San Juan River near the Navajo River confluence, then to the well-known thermal springs at the bend of the San Juan below Wolf Creek Pass. Macomb called the springs Pagosa, a Ute word meaning "boiling water." Later promotion brochures proclaimed it "the largest, hottest spring in the world." From there the party proceeded west along the foothills of the San Juan Mountains, creating a path still used in the present — now it is designated U.S. Highway 160. The men camped one night on a stream they named the Nutria (Spanish word meaning "otter") and the following day wound around the sheer north side of the Chimney Rock cuesta to make a ford of the upper Piedra River. The imposing Chimney Rock formation was sketched by geologist John Newberry. Later, artist J. J. Young produced a lithograph from Newberry's drawing but greatly exaggerated the space between the chimneys. Newberry, who wrote detailed descriptions of other prehis-toric remains seen during the survey, failed to note those on the head-lands of the Piedra. Newberry did comment upon a Capote encampment the men passed twelve miles west of Pagosa Springs, where women were busy collecting and drying berries and cleaning and dressing hides. Other Ute camps were seen on the Piedra and Pine terraces. Perhaps one was on Stollsteimer Mesa, where Roberts in 1923 reported finding tepee poles and rings and a scattering of glass beads.

The future was crashing in upon the Southern Utes in the early 1860s. It began when Charles Baker discovered gold in the highest San Juans, sparking the growth of the nearby boom camp of Silverton. A more inaccessible spot could hardly be imagined. Range after range of the continent's most rugged mountains blocked a direct route from the towns just getting established along eastern Colorado foothills. Baker saw that the best negotiable gateway for the throng he anticipated would soon come to cash in on his strike was a route long familiar to the Utes. It ran along the broad valley east of the mountainous blockade of the San Juans, around its southern tip, to the avenue leading north provided by the Chama drainage. A man of enterprise, Baker carved out a wagon road from Abiquiu to Pagosa and on to Devil Creek behind the Chimney Rock battlement, built the first bridges across the Piedra and Pine, and then made a rocky trail beside the gushing Animas up to his mining camp. The route was formally chartered by the first Colorado state legislature on January 16, 1877, to be known as the Animas City, Pagosa Springs, and Conejos Wagon Road. Rates were set at one dollar for each vehicle and span of horses. Baker staked out housesites at the thermal springs to sell to those who might not want to endure frigid winters at

10,000 feet. The wilderness was to be tamed, at tremendous cost to those who had been there first and preferred to have it remain as it was.

The Capotes were then living in the Chama area, raising a few goats and existing off government rations, but they did not take kindly to the developments going on in other parts of their territory. They so frequently attacked men bound for the Animas gold fields that the government was forced to prohibit prospectors from entering the San Juans. Nevertheless, the lure of gold outweighed risks and illegalities, and the traffic continued. What appeared to be a compromise of sorts was reached in 1874. In that year Congress ratified the Brunot Agreement calling for the Utes to cede the mountaintops to the United States. This area amounted to one-quarter of the traditional Ute range, or some twelve million acres. The tribe retained lower lands to the south and west, which miners still had to cross to get to the shafts. Expectedly, confrontations and racial hatred mounted. Four years later Fort Lewis, no more than a few tents pitched along a raw dirt street, was placed at Pagosa Springs to keep the peace. It was on land claimed by the Capotes. Nonetheless, an atmosphere of cordiality reigned in a July 4th celebration at the springs, with tepees nudged against tents. With settlement expanding westward, in 1881 Fort Lewis was moved to the La Plata drainage.

From the time Colorado was declared a territory in 1861, there was loud agitation to rid the region of the Utes. Precious minerals and hidden valleys promising fertile fields were there for exploitation by immigrant whites, not Native Americans. Feeling that a relatively small tribe should not have exclusive use of such a boundless territory, the government set aside two Indian reservations within the state. This measure did not satisfy those who wanted the Utes out entirely. Matters came to a head after an agent at the White River agency and six of his staff were brutally murdered and the agent's wife and daughter were kidnapped by Utes in the so-called Meeker Massacre. An army unit precipitated the tragedy by marching into Indian land against treaty provisions. Regardless, all the northern Ute bands then were banished to a reservation in northeastern Utah. The Capotes and Moaches fared better. They were allowed to stay in Colorado on a Pine River reservation incorporating

728,320 acres of original Capote range. A few years later the Wimi-nuches chose to settle on a more westerly reservation.

The opening up of the San Juan mining district stimulated the movement of Hispanos out of the Tierra Amarilla–Chama area into the upper San Juan district. These newcomers were primarily teamsters plying a new toll road built from the New Mexican settlements down Canyon Largo on the west side of the Continental Divide to the San Juan River. A further influx of Hispanos came through the construction of the narrow gauge Denver, Rio Grande and Western Railroad, running from Antonito in the San Luis Valley over Cumbres Pass, then westward along the mesas falling away from the high mountains, to the San Juan River and eventually on to Durango. The tracks, laid across the Southern Ute Indian Reservation without official sanction, brought in another element: Hispanic sheepherders who could now get their animals from pasture to market. One prominent arrival was Antonio Archuleta, rancher and member of the young Colorado legislature, who proposed a county in the new area. It was established and named after him. A bit of northern New Mexico ambience was transplanted to another frontier when Hispanos built compounds of gable-roofed jacal or adobe structures recalling those in the Chama area, with a welter of outbuildings, grist mills, corn cribs, privies, and corrals. By 1880 there were at least eight tiny Hispanic communities trying to put down roots along the San Juan drainages. Once more the region evolved as an isolated refuge removed from the scenes of major action, a backwater where survival depended on the subsistence economy of orchards, kitchen gardens, root cellars, and sheep. Inbred and marginal in every sense, these Hispanos depended for solidarity upon familial and spiritual bonds that became more conservative and unchanging through time.

Meanwhile, because the Utes' hunting and gathering possibilities were being eliminated by the march of civilization, the U.S. government returned to the old idea of making farmers out of them. In 1886 a program to give Southern Utes land under a severalty arrangement was begun. A family could acquire an individual allotment of 160 acres. The prospects for the success of this plan were in doubt, not only because private ownership of land was foreign to the Ute way of thinking but also because farming remained anathema to them. By 1891 only thirty-five families

Hispanic family on the move from northern New Mexico to southern Colorado, probably in the late nineteenth century. *Courtesy Colorado Historical Society.*

A Ute and his buggy in front of his teepee, with no farmland in sight. *Courtesy Center for Southwest Studies, Fort Lewis College.*

Ute house and brush *ramada* that may have been either copied after those of the early Hispanic settlers in the upper San Juan area or actually built by them. *Courtesy Center for Southwest Studies, Fort Lewis College.*

Hispanic Penitente rites taking place in the upper San Juan area. Men in foreground carry whips used for self-flagellation. *Courtesy Center for Southwest Studies, Fort Lewis College.*

had begun to farm. Others took some land but hired the newly arrived Hispanos to clear it, dig irrigation ditches, build houses, and raise crops on shares or leases. Lands the Utes did not use were considered surplus and were opened to whites. This furthered the Hispanic homestead style of life and led to a checkerboard pattern of non-Indian holdings within the reservation. Eventually, 523,079 acres allotted to the Utes were sold to others.

The Piedra Valley fell into the category of surplus lands. At its juncture with Nutria Creek, Rubio Gallegos built a one-room cabin of hand-hewn logs chinked with clay and farmed the bottomlands. Two Martínez families took homesteads near Stollsteimer Mesa. Juan Román Gurule staked out a plot on the central Piedra. Antonio María Abeyta moved to Yellowjacket, west of the pinnacles. These and other neighbors participated in Penitente affairs at a *morada* erected within sight of Chimney Rock and Companion Rock. Each month their womenfolk prepared a small Catholic chapel at the junction of the Piedra River and

Utes dipping sheep, probably at the Arboles vat. *Courtesy Colorado Historical Society.*

Nutria Creek for a Mass conducted by a priest who rode there in a buggy from Arboles, a railroad town with a large sheep-dipping vat used by all the herders in the region.

The federal government absorbed three unclaimed townships along the northern rim of the Ute reservation into its forest- and land-management holdings. Included was the Chimney Rock district. An ancient Native American community and possible shrine was to become an Anglo-American tourist attraction.

Immigrants other than Hispanos also moved into the region. Most notable among them was Christian Stollsteimer, a German who developed a large ranch on the Nutria. Later this stream was renamed Stollsteimer in his honor. The *La Plata Miner* in 1880 reported, "Mr. Stollsteimer is one of the most successful stock men in southwestern Colorado, and has immense herds of cattle and sheep which roam over the mesas and foothills to the west of the San Juan river." Stollsteimer soon allied himself with the Hispanos and Indians. His seven children married into Spanish-American families, and he himself served for a time as agent to the Southern Utes and Jicarilla Apaches. During this tenure, he sought to drive Anglos out of the area.

However, Anglos were not to be denied the right to move along the expanding frontier. In the late 1870s Eli Perkins and John Peterson settled near where the Baker bridge spanned the upper Piedra. Shortly they had Henry Freeman, J. R. Scott, and R. A. Howe as neighbors. There was an undercurrent of racial tension. Relations between Utes and Hispanos generally were friendly, occasionally leading to intermarriages, but clashes between Utes and Anglos were frequent. One Ute, who had taken the name of George Washington, claimed land to the east of Chimney Rock; he permitted Hispanic sheepherders to cross it freely but charged Anglos a fee. Settlers Scott and Howe retaliated by putting up signs in English warning Indians to stay off their property. Utes wandering through the valley could not have read the signs, nor would they have heeded them. To them, this was *their* place.

The Twin War Gods, enshrined in stone, looked down.

SELECTED REFERENCES

Adams, E. Charles
  1975   Causes of Prehistoric Settlement Systems in the Lower Piedra District,
         Colorado. Ph.D. dissertation, University of Colorado, Boulder.

Bertram, Jack B., and Nancy S. Hammack
  1991   Half-Baked Ovens. Further Excavations at the Oven Site, LA4169, Navajo
         Reservoir. Paper presented at annual meeting of the Society for American
         Archaeology, New Orleans.

Buckles, William G.
  1968   Archaeology in Colorado Historic Tribes: Utes. *Southwestern Lore*, Vol. 34,
         No. 3, 53–67.

Carlson, Roy L.
  1964   Two Rosa Phase Pit Houses. *Southwestern Lore*, Vol. 29, No. 4, 69–76.

Dittert, A. E.
  1958   Preliminary Archaeological Investigations in the Navajo Project Area of
         Northwestern New Mexico. *Museum of New Mexico Papers in Anthropology*,
         No. 1, Santa Fe.

Dittert, A. E., J. J. Hester, and Frank W. Eddy
  1961   An Archaeological Survey of the Navajo Reservoir District, Northwestern
         New Mexico. *School of American Research and Museum of New Mexico
         Monograph*, No. 23, Santa Fe.

Dittert, A. E., Frank W. Eddy, and Beth L. Dickey
  1 63   Evidences of Early Ceramic Phases in the Navajo Reservoir District. *El
         Palacio*, Vol. 70, 5–12.

Eddy, Frank W.
  1961   Excavations at Los Pinos Phase Sites in the Navajo Reservoir District.
         Museum of New Mexico Papers in Anthropology, No. 4, Santa Fe.
  1972   Culture Ecology and the Prehistory of the Navajo Reservoir District. *South-
         western Lore*, Vol. 38, Nos. 1–2, 1–75.
  1973   Pueblo Settlement Adaptations in the Upper San Juan Basin of New Mexico
         and Colorado, A.D. 1–1125. Paper presented at annual meeting of the Society
         for American Archaeology, San Francisco.
  1977   Archaeological Investigations at Chimney Rock Mesa: 1970–1972. *Memoirs
         of the Colorado Archaeological Society*, No. 1.

1990   Recent Archaeological Research at Chimney Rock Mesa, Southwestern Colorado. In *From Chimney Rock to Chaco,* papers of the Chimney Rock Archaeological Conference, Fort Lewis College, Durango. Forthcoming.

Ellis, Florence M.
    1973   A Thousand Years of the Pueblo Sun-Moon-Star Calendar. Paper presented at annual meeting of the American Association for the Advancement of Science, Mexico City.
    1988   *From Drought to Drought: Gallina Culture Patterns.* Vol 1. Sunstone Press, Santa Fe.

Ellis, Florence M. and J. J. Brody
    1964   Ceramic Stratigraphy and Tribal History at Taos Pueblo. *American Antiquity,* Vol. 29, No. 3, 316–327.

Ford, Richard, Albert H. Schroeder, and Stewart L. Peckham
    1972   Three Perspectives on Pueblo Prehistory. In *New Perspectives on the Pueblos.* Edited by Alfonso Ortiz. University of New Mexico Press, Albuquerque, 22–40.

Gilbert, Elizabeth X.
    1961   A Pithouse Village on the San Juan River, New Mexico. *Southwestern Lore,* Vol. 27, No. 1, 9–16.

Hibben, Frank C.
    1948   The Gallina Architectural Forms. *American Antiquity,* Vol. 14, No. 1, 32–36.
    1949   The Pottery of the Gallina Complex. *American Antiquity,* Vol. 14, No. 3, 194–202.

Jeancon, Jean Allard
    1922   *Archaeological Research in the Northeastern San Juan Basin of Colorado During the Summer of 1921.* Edited by Frank H. H. Roberts. State Historical and Natural History Society of Colorado and the University of Denver, Denver, 1–31.
    1924   Archaeological and Ethnological Research During the Year of 1924. Unpublished manuscript at the Colorado Historical Society, Denver.
    1925   Archaeological and Ethnological Research During the Year of 1925. Unpublished manuscript at the Colorado Historical Society, Denver.

Jeancon, Jean Allard, and Frank H. H. Roberts
    1923   Archaeological Research in the Northeastern Basin of Colorado During the Summer of 1922. *Colorado Magazine,* Vol. 1, No. 1, 11–36; No. 2, 65–70; No. 3, 108–118; No. 4, 163–173; No. 5, 213–224; No. 6, 260–276; No. 7, 301–307.

Kane, Allen E.
    1986   Organizational Models for Northern Chacoan Outlier Communities. Paper presented at the Third Anasazi Conference, Monument Valley, Arizona.

Lange, Charles H.

    1956   The Evans Site and the Archaeology of the Gallina Region, New Mexico. *El Palacio*, Vol. 63, No. 3, 72–90.

LeGare, David

    1990   Piedra/Gallina Analogs. In *From Chimney Rock to Chaco*, papers of the Chimney Rock Archaeological Conference, Fort Lewis College, Durango. Forthcoming.

Lister, Robert H., Stephen J. Hallisy, Margeret H. Kane, and George E. McLellan

    1970   Site 5LP11, a Pueblo I Site Near Ignacio, Colorado. *Southwestern Lore*, Vol. 35, No. 4, 57–67.

Malville, J. McKim, and Claudia Putnam

    1989   *Prehistoric Astronomy in the Southwest*. Johnson Books, Boulder.

Marsh, Charles S.

    1982   *People of the Shining Mountains*. Pruett Publishers, Boulder.

Marshall, Michael L., John R. Stein, Richard W. Loose, and Judith E. Novotny

    1979   *Anasazi Communities of the San Juan Basin*. Department of the Interior, Heritage Conservation and Recreation Service, Santa Fe.

Motter, John M.

    1984   *Pagosa Country: The First Fifty Years*. Privately printed, Pagosa Springs, Colorado.

Newren, Marcia T., Peter McKenna, and W. James Judge

    1990   The Place of Chimney Rock in the Chaco Network. In *From Chimney Rock to Chaco*, papers of the Chimney Rock Archaeological Conference, Fort Lewis College, Durango. Forthcoming.

Parsons, Elsie Clews

    1939   *Pueblo Indian Religion*. 2 vols. University of Chicago Press, Chicago.

Powers, Robert P., William B. Gillespie, and Stephen H. Lekson

    1983   *The Outlier Survey: A Regional View of Settlement in the San Juan Basin*. National Park Service, Division of Cultural Research, Albuquerque.

Prescott, William H.

    1844   *History of the Conquest of Mexico*. Random House, New York. Modern Library reprint.

Roberts, Frank H. H.

    1922   Report on the Work of the 1922 Season in the Piedra Parada Archaeological Field. *University of Denver Bulletin*, Vol. 23, No. 9.

    1925   Report on an Archaeological Reconnaissance in Southwestern Colorado in the Summer of 1923. *Colorado Magazine*, Vol. 2, No. 2, 3–84.

    1930   Early Pueblo Ruins in the Piedra District, Southwestern Colorado. *Bureau of American Ethnology Bulletin*, No. 96.

Schaafsma, Polly
  1963   Rock Art in the Navajo Reservoir District. *Museum of New Mexico Papers in Anthropology*, No. 7.

Schroeder, Albert H.
  1965   A Brief History of the Southern Utes. *Southwestern Lore*, Vol. 30, No. 4, 53–78.

Sullivan, Mary
  1990   Chimney Rock Ceramics. In *From Chimney Rock to Chaco*, papers of the Chimney Rock Archaeological Conference, Fort Lewis College, Durango. Forthcoming.
  1990b   Clusters of Clay: A Compositional Analysis of Ceramics From Chimney Rock. M.A. thesis, University of Colorado, Boulder.

Swadesh, Frances Leon
  1966   Hispanic Americans of the Ute Frontier From the Chama Valley to the San Juan Basin, 1694–1960. Ph.D. dissertation, University of Colorado, Boulder.

Thompson, G. C.
  1972   Southern Ute Lands, 1848–1899. *Center for Southwest Studies Occasional Paper*, No. 1, Fort Lewis College, Durango.

Truell, Marcia
  1975   1972 Archaeological Explorations at the Ravine Site, Chimney Rock, Colorado. M.A. thesis, University of Colorado, Boulder.

Tucker, Gordon C.
  1981   The Prehistoric Settlement System on Chimney Rock Mesa, South-Central Colorado, A.D. 925–1125. Ph.D. dissertation, University of Colorado, Boulder.

Vivian, R. Gwinn
  1990   *The Chacoan Prehistory of the San Juan Basin*. Academic Press, New York.

INDEX

Abiquiu, 113, 120–23
Adams, E. Charles, 68–69
Albino Village, 49(fig.)
Allison, 30
American Museum of Natural History, 11
Anasazi, 43, 48, 56, 60–68, 73, 83–84, 87–89, 98, 106, 116–17, 119
Animas City, Pagosa Springs, and Conejos Wagon Road, 123
Animas River, 11, 29, 52, 113, 123–24
Arboles, 31, 61, 129
Arboles Phase, 61(fig.), 67–69, 82–83. See also Pueblo II, early; Sanchez Site
Archaic period, 46–47
Archuleta, Antonio, 125
Aztec Indians, 10
Aztec Ruins, 11, 17, 26, 100

Baker, Charles, 123
Basketmaker, 11, 20, 41, 48, 59
Basketmaker II, 47–52
Basketmaker III, 33, 35, 53–60, 70
Basketry, 11, 48, 51, 53, 58, 62, 88, 114
Beans, 35, 63, 66, 85, 120
Bone implements, 13, 51, 58
Brunot Agreement, 124
Bureau of American Ethnology, 12, 35
Burials, 21–22, 24(fig.), 38, 41, 51, 55, 63, 67, 72, 119

Canyon de Chelly, 120
Capote, Lake, 79
Capote Ute Indians, 113–15, 119–24
Carson, Kit, 122
Cat Creek Ridge, 68
Causeway, 14, 81
Chaco Archeological Protection Site System, xi
Chaco Canyon: National Monument, xi; area of, 11, 17, 32, 35, 38, 64–66, 91, 99–100, 104, 107–108; Chaco culture, influence of, 17, 21, 26, 99–100, 103–106 Chaco Phenomenon, xi, 100, 108
Chama River, 113, 120–25

Chimney Rock: cuesta, 3–4, 11, 13–14, 19(fig.), 31, 34(fig.), 35(fig.), 74d(fig.), 81(fig.), 86, 99; district, 5, 9, 22, 114, 121, 123, 129; indigenous structures, on mesa, 13–14, 87–98; pinnacles, 1–2, 12, 31, 52, 68, 74a-c, g-h(figs.), 113, 116, 128; pueblo, xi, 12, 14–15, 16(fig.), 17–18, 25–26, 25(fig.), 32, 43, 74e-g(figs.), 76(fig.), 99–108, 99(fig.); pueblo, stabilization of, 27, 75–76, 76(fig.), 77(fig.), 80(fig.); terrace sites, 12, 18–20, 23, 25, 32–33, 83, 84(fig.); village clusters, 70–83, 87
Chimney Rock Archeological Area, xi, 2(map), 43(map), 80, 87
Chuska Mountains, 104
Cists, 11, 49, 54(fig.), 55–56, 58, 65, 70, 71(fig.), 72(fig.), 83, 94, 98, 102
Coal Hill, 31
Colorado Historical Society. See State Historical and Natural History Society
Colorado Plateau, 3, 5, 54, 63, 86, 109; aboriginal cultures on, 10–11, 24, 33, 42, 46, 60, 66, 84, 104, 116
Comanche Indians, 114–15
Companion Rock, xi, 2–3, 12, 18, 52, 68, 113, 116, 128
Complete Archaeological Service Associates, 70
Corn, 13, 35, 45–46, 48, 51, 58, 63, 66, 69, 80, 82, 85, 120
Corn-goddess fetish, 63, 66
Cremation, 18, 22
Cumbres Pass, 125

Dance plaza, 25, 32, 34(fig.), 38
Denver, Rio Grande and Western Railroad, 125
Devil Creek, 3–4, 13, 31, 83, 123
Dinetah, 115, 117
Dittert, A. E., Jr., 43
Dog burial, 52, 55, 63
Domínguez and Escalante expedition, 120
Durango, 23, 47, 52, 125

Eddy, Frank, xii, 55, 70, 72, 75, 86–87, 94, 95, 95(fig.), 98–102
Effigy, 24(fig.), 58, 63, 66, 117
Embudo, 120

Feather holder, 98, 107(fig.), 108
Fewkes, Jesse Walter, 12, 22
Fort Lewis, 124
Fort Sumner, 120

Gailina, 21, 70, 85, 109
Gobernador, 60, 63, 85, 109, 115, 119
Great House. *See* Chimney Rock pueblo; Outliers
Great Kiva, 99–100
Great Kiva, Site 5AA88, Mound 17, 94–95, 96(fig.), 97(fig.), 98, 100, 102–103
Guardhouse, 14, 24, 76, 81(fig.), 107

Hammack, Nancy and Larry, 70–71
Harlan ranch site, 19(fig.), 23, 33
Haystack Mountain, 30
Hispanos, 28, 35, 65, 122, 125, 126(fig.), 128–30
Hopi Indians, 11, 107, 114, 120

Ignacio, 23, 80

Jacal structures, 30, 37(fig.), 41, 51, 61, 65, 68–69, 78–80, 83, 90, 108
Jeancon, J. A., 10–23, 25(fig.), 26–27, 31–35, 38, 70, 75, 83, 99–101
Jemez Plateau, 20, 85
Jemez Pueblo, 31, 109, 113, 115
Jewelry, 17(fig.), 52, 58, 63
Jicarilla Apache Indians, 115, 129

Kane, Allan, 104
Keresan language, 103
Kidder, Alfred V., 22
Kivas, 15, 16, 24–26, 25(fig.), 35, 38, 66, 79(fig.), 80(fig.), 98–103, 108

La Plata River, 64, 116, 124
Largo Canyon, 109, 115, 125
Lewis shale, 88
Lister, Robert H., xii, 78
Los Pinos Phase, 47–52, 55, 59. *See also* Basketmaker II
Lowry Ruin, 103
Lunar standstill, 106, 108

McCauley, Lt. C.A.H., 9
Macomb, Capt. John N., 122
Maize. *See* Corn.

Malville, McKim, 105–106
Martin, Paul, 35
Meeker Massacre, 124
Mesa Verde, 10, 20, 23, 27, 32, 65, 84, 91, 108
Mesa Verde Research Center, 75
Mexico, 10, 21, 56
Moache Ute Indians, 114–15, 122, 124
Mogollon, 53, 56
Montezuma Mesa, 30
Museum of New Mexico, 43, 46

Navajo Indians, 29, 31, 45(fig.), 46, 54(fig.), 65, 75, 117(fig.); Pueblo influence on, 115–17, 119
Navajo Reservoir: archaeological project, 43, 44(map), 46, 52, 59, 64, 66, 68, 69, 70, 72, 75; district, xii, 43–44, 44(map), 46, 49(fig.), 52–53, 59, 60–61, 66, 68–69, 73, 86, 117(fig.)
Navajo River, 122
Newberry, John, 123
Nusbaum, Jesse L., 27
Nutria Creek, 123, 128–29

Obsidian, 85
Ojo Caliente, 120
Old Spanish Trail, 121–22
Outliers, 100, 103–104, 107–108
Oven. *See* Cists
Oven Site, 70, 71(fig.), 72(fig). *See also* Sambrito Village

Pagosa Junction, 23
Pagosa Springs, 10, 13, 22–23, 28, 122–24
Paiute Indians, 114
Piedra Parada, 1, 120
Paleo-Indian period, 46–47
Palmer, J. S., 11–13, 22
Pargin ranch, 12
Parking Lot Site, 93(fig.), 94(fig.), 95(fig.)
Payan Corrugated pottery, 33, 68, 85(fig.)
Pecos Classification, 47
Pecos Conference, 33, 38
Penitente, 128(fig.)
Petersen Mesa, 4, 33(fig.)
Pictured Cliff sandstone, 3, 88
Piedra Phase, 64–67, 69, 80, 83, 98. *See also* Pueblo I, late Piedra River, 3–4, 18, 23, 27, 38, 43, 56, 60–61, 65, 67, 70, 80, 83, 84, 86, 98, 106, 116, 123, 128; district, 22, 33, 41, 69, 80, 100, 123; valley, 1, 9–10, 12, 31, 74d(fig.), 76, 79, 80, 82, 83(fig.), 115, 121, 128
Pine River, 1, 23, 43, 45, 47, 49(fig.), 52, 80, 123

Pipes, 58, 63
Pithouses: 19–20, 23–24, 30–33, 38, 41, 48–49, 49(fig.), 50(fig.), 53–55, 59–60, 65, 67, 69, 72, 78–80, 83, 90–91, 90(fig.), 93; above-ground style, 11–13, 89–90, 96, 109
Plaza Grande, 32–33, 33(fig.)
Pottery: occupation indicators, 9, 13, 15, 18, 30; styles of, 20–21, 24, 26(fig.), 33, 38; Basketmaker II brown ware, 51; Basketmaker III brown ware, 56, 57(figs.), 58; Chaco ware, 105; Navajo ware, 116–17; Pueblo I ware, 39(figs.), 40(figs.), 61–62; Early Pueblo II ware, 39(figs.), 40(figs.), 68, 84, 88, 98; Ute ware, 114
Pre-Pueblo, 30–31, 35. *See also* Pueblo I
Prescott, William H., 10
Projectile points, 41, 46, 58, 62, 79, 84, 114
Pueblo Bonito, 11, 17
Pueblo culture, 20, 48, 52, 59, 116
Pueblo Indians, 2, 10–11, 18, 41, 45, 106, 109, 113, 115; refugees, 30–31, 116–17, 118(figs.), 119(figs.), 121
Pueblo I: early, 35, 36(fig.), 38, 39(figs.), 40(figs.), 41, 59–64; late, 64–67, 80, 83(fig.). *See also* Piedra Phase; Rosa Phase
Pueblo II: early, 24, 35, 37(fig.), 38(fig.), 39(figs.), 40(figs.), 61(figs.), 67–68, 83, 83(fig.), 84(fig.). *See also* Arboles Phase
Pyramid Mountain, 91, 93

Renaud, E. B., 12
Rivera, Juan Maria, 120
Roads, 100–101, 104, 108
Roberts, Frank H.H., Jr., 33, 66; on Chimney Rock excavations, 12, 23, 70, 76, 83, 104; on San Juan survey, 27–31, 28(fig.), 100; on Stollsteimer excavations, 35, 37–38, 41–42, 65, 68, 78, 123
Rock art, 31, 45–46, 79, 114, 117
Rosa Phase, 59–64, 61(fig.), 69. *See also* Pueblo I, early

Salmon Ruin, 104
Sambrito Creek, 54, 65
Sambrito Phase, 53–60, 56(fig.), 57(fig.), 62, 72. *See also* Basketmaker III
Sambrito Village, 53(fig.), 54(fig.), 59, 71. *See also* Oven Site
Sanchez Site, 61(fig.)
Sandoval Mesa, 67
Sangre de Cristo Mountains, 109
San Juan Basin, xi–xii, 2(map), 3, 9–10, 13, 19, 32–33, 43, 46, 50, 56, 59, 68–69, 80, 83, 105, 108, 120, 125

San Juan Basin Archaeological Society, xii
San Juan Mountains, 1, 3, 9, 47, 74c(fig.), 64, 109, 113, 120, 122–24
San Juan National Forest, xi–xii, 27, 75
San Juan National Forest Association, xii
San Juan River, 1, 4, 10, 23, 27–28, 30–31, 41, 43–47, 53–54, 58, 60–61, 63, 65, 67, 70, 76, 80, 98, 103, 109, 113, 115–16, 119–22, 125
San Luis Valley, 114, 120, 122, 125
School of American Research, 43
Shabikleschee, 66
Signaling station, 18, 30, 100
Sipapu, 16, 60, 63
Site 5AA83, 78, 99(fig.). *See also* Chimney Rock, pueblo
Site 5AA86. *See* Parking Lot Site
Site 5AA88, 89(fig.), 90(fig.), 91(fig.), 92(figs.), 96–97
Site 5AA88, Mound 17. *See* Great Kiva
Site 5AA92, 82(fig.)
Site LA3017, 45(fig.)
Site LA4071, 117(fig.)
Site LA4169. *See* Oven Site; Sambrito Village
Site LA4269. *See* Albino Village
Solar solstice, 106
Southern Ute Indians. *See* Ute Indians
Southern Ute Indian Reservation, xi, 35, 68, 79–80, 125F 129
Spaniards, 1, 9, 30–31, 113–16, 120–21
Squash, 47, 63, 66
Squaw Creek, 10
State Historical and Natural History Society, 10, 14(fig.), 18, 22–23, 27, 32, 35, 75, 104
Stockade, 60, 66–67, 87
Stollsteimer, Christian, 129
Stollsteimer Creek, 4, 38, 129
Stollsteimer Mesa, 31–33, 32(fig.), 35, 36(fig.), 37(fig.), 39(figs.), 40(figs.), 67–68, 78–79, 123, 128
Stollsteimer Valley, 86
Stone circle, 30, 100
Stone implements, 13, 15, 30, 46, 51, 55, 58, 62, 66, 84, 89, 92(fig.), 98, 105, 114, 116, 119

Tamuche, 121
Taos, 121–22
Taos Pueblo, 109
Taylor, Mount, 120
Tewa language, 103
Tierra Amarilla land grant, 122, 125
Timber: as trade item, 104, 108

Tower, 20, 33, 35(fig.), 83, 106
Trade, 17, 21, 59, 62–63, 66, 84
Tree-ring dates, 60; Chimney Rock pueblo, 101, 102(fig.), 103, 106; Great Kiva, 98, 103
Trujillo, 29
Turquoise, 24, 104–105
Twin War Gods, 2–3, 5, 18, 45(fig.), 46, 105, 109, 130

University of Colorado, xii, 68, 75, 80, 87
University of Denver, 12, 22
University of New Mexico, xi
Upper Colorado River Storage Project, 43

Ute Indians, 9, 23, 31, 35, 68, 78, 114–16, 119–21, 123–26, 127(fig.), 128, 129(fig.), 130. *See also* Capote Ute Indians; Moache Ute Indians; Wiminuche Ute Indians

Washington, George, 130
Wetherill, Richard, 10–11
White River agency, 124
Wiminuche Ute Indians, 113, 125
Wolf Creek Pass, 13, 122

Yellowjacket Creek, 9, 128
Young, J. J., 123